UNCLE TOM'S CABIN

Evil, Affliction,
and Redemptive Love

Twayne's Masterwork Studies
Robert Lecker, General Editor

UNCLE TOM'S CABIN

*Evil, Affliction,
and Redemptive Love*

Josephine Donovan

TWAYNE PUBLISHERS • BOSTON
A Division of G. K. Hall & Co.

Twayne's Masterworks Series No. 63

Copyright 1991 by G. K. Hall & Co.
All rights reserved.
Published by Twayne Publishers
A division of G. K. Hall & Co.
70 Lincoln Street
Boston, Massachusetts 02111

Copyediting supervised by Barbara Sutton.
Book production by Janet Z. Reynolds.
Typeset by Huron Valley Graphics, Inc., Ann Arbor, Michigan.

First published 1991.
10 9 8 7 6 5 4 3 2 1 (hc)
10 9 8 7 6 5 4 3 2 1 (pb)

Printed and bound in the United States of America.

Library of Congress Cataloging-in-Publication Data

Donovan, Josephine, 1941–
    Uncle Tom's cabin : evil, affliction, and redemptive love /
Josephine Donovan.
        p.   cm. — (Twayne's masterwork studies ; no. 63)
    Includes bibliographical references and index.
    ISBN 0-8057-8095-5. — ISBN 0-8057-8140-4 (pbk.)
    1. Stowe, Harriet Beecher, 1811–1896. Uncle Tom's cabin.
2. Slavery and slaves in literature.   3. Plantation life in
literature.   4. Redemption in literature.   5. Evil in literature.
6. Love in literature.   I. Title.   II. Series.
PS2954.U6D66   1991
813'.3—dc20   90-44091
                                                      CIP

For My Students

Hers was the word for the hour
—FREDERICK DOUGLASS

Contents

Note on the References and Acknowledgments

In this study all references are to *Uncle Tom's Cabin: Or Life among the Lowly,* edited by Ann Douglas (New York: Penguin, 1981), a paperback reprint of the 1962 Harvard University Press reissue of the first edition text, edited by Kenneth S. Lynn. Page numbers in parentheses follow citations. The Penguin edition is the most accessible modern reprint of the first edition of the novel. It does, however, differ from the first edition in that it does not include the author's preface and it does include a title for chapter 8, which is not in the first edition. There are also a few typos in the Penguin edition that are not in the original 1852 edition.

I would like to take this opportunity to thank the University of Maine for a 1989 Summer Faculty Research grant and for release time that facilitated completion of this book. In addition, I would like to express my gratitude to the following for their contributions to this project: Barbara White, Marilyn Emerick, Elaine Ayer, and Robert Lecker; and Lewis DeSimone and Barbara Sutton, editors at G. K. Hall, with whom I have had the pleasure of working on many other projects and from whom I have learned much.

Chronology:
Harriet Beecher Stowe's Life and Works

1811   Harriet Elizabeth Beecher born 14 June to Lyman Beecher, a Congregationalist minister, and Roxana Foote Beecher, of a Tory Episcopalian family, the seventh of nine children, in Litchfield, Connecticut.

1816   Harriet's mother dies 25 September, a devastating event Harriet later sees as the most important of her childhood.

1817   Lyman remarries, Harriet Porter, of Portland, Maine in October or November. The couple has three children.

1819   In a letter Lyman observes, "Harriet is a genius. I would give a hundred dollars if she was a boy. She is as odd as she is intelligent and studious."

1822   Alexander Metcalf Fisher, fiancé of Catharine E. Beecher, Harriet's older sister, dies 22 April. The event precipitates a religious crisis in the Beecher sisters and is treated fictionally in *The Minister's Wooing*.

1823   In May Catharine Beecher founds Hartford Female Seminary, which Harriet attends and later teaches in (1824–32). "Can the Immortality of the Soul Be Proved by the Light of Nature?" Harriet's first work, a theological treatise.

1825   Writes *Cleon*, a tragedy in blank verse, about a Christian convert in Nero's court. First conversion experience in November.

1826   Lyman becomes pastor of Boston's Hanover Street Church in March; household moves there.

1829   Becomes full-time teacher at Hartford Female Seminary in January; her subjects are rhetoric and composition.

1831   Catharine Beecher's anti-Calvinist treatise, *Elements of Mental and Moral Philosophy.*

1832   Lyman becomes president of Lane Theological Seminary in Cincinnati. Catharine starts Western Female Institute there with Harriet on the faculty and her chief assistant.

1833   First publication, "Modern Uses of Language," *Western Monthly*, March. First book, *Primary Geography for Children, on an Improved Plan*, published in Cincinnati. In summer visits estate in Washington, Kentucky, with friend Mary Dutton, who later recalls, "Harriet did not seem to notice anything that happened, but sat much of the time as though abstracted in thought. . . . Afterwards, however, in reading 'Uncle Tom,' I recognized scene after scene of that visit portrayed with the most minute fidelity, and knew at once where the material for that portion of the story had been gathered."

1834   In February publishes first story, "Isabelle and Her Sister Kate, and Their Cousin," in *Western Monthly,* under pseudonym May. Also in February slavery debates are held at Lane Theological Seminary on topic "Ought the Slaveholding States to Abolish Slavery Immediately?" In April wins $50 award for her story "Uncle Lot," published as "A New England Sketch" in *Western Monthly,* edited by James Hall. Story is eventually retitled "Uncle Tim" for the *Mayflower* collection. In October hears story in Ripley, Ohio, about fugitive slave woman who crossed the Ohio River on blocks of ice, the basis for the Eliza episode in *Uncle Tom's Cabin*.

1836   Marries Calvin E. Stowe, Professor of Biblical Criticism and Oriental Literature at Lane Theological Seminary, on 6 January. Angelina Grimké, *Appeal to the Christian Women of the South*.

1837   Catharine Beecher, *Essay on Slavery*. In November abolitionist Elijah P. Lovejoy killed by mob in Alton, Illinois; Edward Beecher, Harriet's brother, narrowly escapes.

1837–1838   Alexander Kinmont lectures in Cincinnati.

1839   Theodore Weld, ed., *American Slavery as It Is: Testimony of a Thousand Witnesses*.

1840   "Free Agency"; refutes Jonathan Edwards on the will.

1843   *The Mayflower; or, Sketches of Scenes and Characters among the Descendants of the Pilgrims*, a collection of fifteen stories, including several, such as "Uncle Tim," "Love *versus* Law," and "Cousin William," that pioneered local color realism in the United States. With a preface by Catharine Beecher; published by Harper & Brothers in New York. Brother George is killed in shotgun accident in July.

Chronology

1840s	Teaches ex-slave children in family school; brother Henry Ward Beecher and Calvin Stowe help fugitive slave woman escape by wagon at night to home of John Van Zandt, an "underground railroad" station—the basis for Eliza's escape in *Uncle Tom's Cabin*.
1845	Second or "true" conversion.
1846	Stays at Dr. Wesselhoeft's water cure sanitorium in Brattleboro, Vermont, from May to March 1847. (Calvin attends June 1848–September 1849.)
1849	Cholera epidemic in Cincinnati in July; one-year-old son Charley dies, along with family's black laundry woman, Aunt Frankie, and family dog, Daisy. Calvin named Collins Professor of Natural and Revealed Religion at Bowdoin College, Brunswick, Maine, a position he holds only briefly. *The Life of Josiah Henson*, slave narrative, one of the sources for *Uncle Tom's Cabin*. (Harriet may have met Henson at the home of her brother Edward in Boston in 1850.)
1850	In May Harriet and three of the children arrive in Brunswick, where in a rented frame house on Federal Street (now an inn), she writes *Uncle Tom's Cabin* (some is written in Calvin's Bowdoin office). Seventh and last child, Charles, later Harriet's first biographer, born 8 July. First piece ("The Freeman's Dream") published in the *National Era*, a Washington, D.C., abolitionist paper, edited by Gamaliel Bailey, 1 August. Fugitive Slave Act passed in September by U.S. Congress. In the fall her sister-in-law, Mrs. Edward Beecher of Boston, urges her to write in opposition to slavery: "Hattie, if I could use a pen as you can, I would write something that would make this whole nation feel what an accursed thing slavery is."
1851	Harriet tells brother Henry in early January, "I have begun a set of sketches in the National Era, to illustrate the cruelty of slavery: I call it Uncle Tom's Cabin" (letter of 22 July 1875). In February has vision of the death of Uncle Tom, in First Parish Church, Brunswick, which allegedly initiates the writing of the novel. (Stowe gave various accounts of the origin of the novel, so this one may be apocryphal.) In 9 March letter to Gamaliel Bailey says that she is preparing "a series of sketches" about slavery for the *National Era*; "it will be ready in two or three weeks" and "may extend through three or four numbers"— the first reliable evidence she had begun work on *Uncle Tom's Cabin*. Notice appears 8 May in *National Era*: "Week after next we propose to commence . . . the publication of a new story by Mrs. H. B. Stowe, the title of which will be, "UNCLE

TOM'S CABIN, OR THE MAN THAT WAS A THING."
Files for copyright in Brunswick 12 May. Chapters 1 and 2 of
Uncle Tom's Cabin; or, Life among the Lowly appear 5 June
on the front page of the *National Era*, beginning the novel's
forty-one-segment serialization over the next nine months.
Writes letter to black abolitionist Frederick Douglass 9 July
asking for factual information for her plantation scenes in
Uncle Tom's Cabin.

1852   *Uncle Tom's Cabin* published as book 20 March by John P.
Jewett & Co. in Boston and Jewett, Procter & Worthington in
Cleveland, in two volumes (312 and 322 pages, respectively).
Chapters 43–45 of *Uncle Tom's Cabin* published 1 April in the
National Era, concluding the serialization of the novel. Jewett
& Co. announce sale of 50,000th copy of the novel 15 May. In
July receives first royalty check, $10,000, for *Uncle Tom's
Cabin*. Also in July Calvin assumes Chair of Sacred Literature
at Andover Theological Seminary in Andover, Massachusetts;
family moves there. First dramatization of *Uncle Tom's Cabin*
(unauthorized) in August; numerous subsequent stage versions
make it the most popular play in American theater history.

1853   First trip to England and Europe March–September. Anniver-
sary of *Uncle Tom's Cabin* 20 March; an estimated 2.5 million
copies have sold worldwide. *The Key to "Uncle Tom's Cabin."
Uncle Sam's Emancipation; Earthly Care a Heavenly Discipline; and Other Sketches.*

1854   *Sunny Memories of Foreign Lands.*

1856   *Dred: A Tale of the Great Dismal Swamp.* Makes second trip
to Europe and Britain from summer to June 1857.

1857   Son Henry, student at Dartmouth, drowns in Hanover, New
Hampshire, 9 July. "The Mourning Veil," story, in first issue of
the *Atlantic Monthly,* November.

1858   Year-long serialization of *The Minister's Wooing* begins in the
Atlantic Monthly in December.

1859   Book publication of *The Minister's Wooing.* Makes third trip
to Europe from August to June 1860.

1861   Son Frederick enlists in the Union Army. Serialization of *The
Pearl of Orr's Island* in the *Independent* from January to April
1862. Serialization of *Agnes of Sorrento* in *Atlantic Monthly*
and *Cornhill* in England from May to April 1862.

1862   Book publications of *The Pearl of Orr's Island: A Story of the
Coast of Maine* and *Agnes of Sorrento.* In November meets

Abraham Lincoln in the White House. He allegedly says, "So this is the little lady who made this great war?"

1863   Emancipation Proclamation 1 January. Harriet hears the announcement in the Boston Music Hall where the audience stands and applauds her. "A Reply to the Affectionate and Christian Address . . . ," an essay on slavery, published in the *Atlantic Monthly* in January. Son Frederick wounded and shell shocked at Gettysburg in July. Calvin retires; family moves to Hartford, Connecticut.

1865   Purchases plantation in Mandarin, Florida, family winter home until 1886. *House and Home Papers,* under pseudonym Christopher Crowfield (originally published in the *Atlantic Monthly* in 1864).

1867   *Religious Poems.*

1868   *The Chimney-Corner,* under pseudonym Christopher Crowfield (originally published in the *Atlantic Monthly* in 1865–66). *Men of Our Times.*

1868–1869   Series of important articles published in *Hearth and Home* on women's rights, animal rights, literary criticism, etc.

1869   *Oldtown Folks. The American Woman's Home* (with Catharine Beecher).

1870   *Lady Byron Vindicated.*

1871   *My Wife and I. Pink and White Tyranny.*

1872   Victoria Woodhull accuses Henry Ward Beecher of adultery with a parishioner, Elizabeth Tilton, in September thus beginning the Beecher–Tilton scandal. *Oldtown Fireside Stories.*

1873   *Palmetto Leaves.*

1874   *Woman in Sacred History.*

1875   *We and Our Neighbors.*

1877   *Footsteps of the Master.*

1878   *Pogonuc People.*

1881   *Sam Lawson's Oldtown Fireside Stories (Oldtown Fireside Stories,* plus five more).

1882   Garden party birthday celebration in June, attended by numerous notables. Frederick Douglass sums up Stowe's achievement: "Hers was the word for the hour."

1886   Calvin dies 6 August.

1888   Harriet's mental faculties deteriorate from this point on.
1896   Dies in Hartford 1 July; buried next to Calvin in the Andover Chapel Cemetery, Andover, Massachusetts.
1910   First film version of *Uncle Tom's Cabin*.

Literary and
Historical Context

1

Background

The world's most powerful political novel was written during a period of revolutionary ferment. The ideals of the French and American Revolutions, especially the doctrine of natural rights and equality before the law, originally extended only to middle-class men, were being claimed for others: workers, women, serfs in Russia, slaves in the United States. The year 1848 saw a series of abortive revolutions throughout Europe and the publication of *The Communist Manifesto*, which called for the dispossessed to rise up against the ruling classes.

Harriet Beecher Stowe was "a radical democrat . . . approaching Karl Marx in her sympathy with a world-wide revolt of the masses."[1] In 1868, looking back on the Civil War, which her book *Uncle Tom's Cabin* had helped precipitate, Stowe revealed once again her identification with the oppressed. It was, she said, a "war for the rights of the working class of society as against the usurpation of privileged aristocracies. . . . *For* us and our cause, all the common working classes of Europe—all that toil and sweat, and are oppressed. Against us, all privileged classes, nobles, princes, bankers and great manufacturers, all who live at ease."[2] No one who has read Stowe's writings—from her personal letters and informal essays to her massive novels—can fail to appreciate her passion for justice.

The decades preceding the publication of *Uncle Tom's Cabin* (1852) were ones of intense political and social agitation in the United States. Reform was in the air. The once dominant religion, Calvinism, was becoming "feminized"—that is, more tolerant and compassionate in its ethic—thanks in part to the writings of the Beechers—especially Harriet's siblings Catharine, Edward, and Henry Ward as well as Harriet herself. An effective antislavery movement was gaining strength, and a women's rights campaign was taking hold. Stowe's novel reflects these historical forces.

Slavery had established a secure foothold in the Americas by the early sixteenth century. Under this system black Africans were captured, transported to the New World (the middle passage) on slave ships, and sold as commodities to white owners. By the nineteenth century slavery was an essential ingredient in the economy of the South. While the African slave trade was abolished in 1808, domestic trade continued until the Emancipation Proclamation in 1863. By 1850 approximately 3 million African-Americans were living under the "peculiar institution" of slavery; by 1860 the number approached 4 million.[3]

Slaves had no legal rights; indeed, they were not considered persons under the Constitution but rather property. Supreme Court Chief Justice Roger Taney summarized their situation in the famous *Dred Scott* decision of 6 March 1857. "Negroes," he wrote, were "a subordinate and inferior class of beings, who had been subjugated by the dominant race, and . . . yet remained subject to their authority, and had no rights or privileges but such as those who held the power and the Government might choose to grant them."[4]

By the 1850s a militant antislavery movement was well under way. William Lloyd Garrison published the first issue of the *Liberator*, an abolitionist journal, in January 1831 and in November of the same year formed the New England Anti-Slavery Society. In the fall of 1850 the antislavery forces received a severe setback, however, when the U.S. Congress passed the Fugitive Slave Law, under which it became

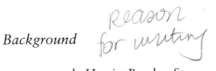

illegal to aid fugitive slaves to escape north. Harriet Beecher Stowe was outraged by this law; it was the immediate precipitant for her writing *Uncle Tom's Cabin*. By this time she had seen slavery firsthand. During her years in Cincinnati she had come to know many ex-slaves personally; some of them and their stories became incorporated in her anti-slavery novel.[5] In addition, several of the issues heatedly discussed by those active in the abolition movement became inscribed in the novel. Of particular importance were the questions of whether to engage in violent or nonviolent tactics and whether to endorse colonization as a solution to the slavery problem. This meant sending blacks back to Africa. Although no African-Americans and few abolitionists supported the idea, it had important adherents, notably Stowe's father, Lyman Beecher, and, for a period, Stowe herself.

Meanwhile, a women's rights movement emerged—in part because of the second-class treatment women received in the abolition movement. Sarah Grimké's *Letters on Equality* (1838), the first major feminist manifesto in the United States, was issued in response to that wrong. In it she recognized that like slaves white women too as a class were oppressed, and she urged that they speak out on their own behalf as well as that of other oppressed groups. Grimké's position was regarded as wildly radical, indeed heretical, by many. A more moderate and conventional approach was proposed by Harriet's sister Catharine. In her *Essay on Slavery* (1837) she rejected political activism for women on the theory that it is socially improper for women to engage in public affairs; instead she urged that women politely persuade men, whom she saw as rightly controlling the public world, to behave in accordance with women's more humanitarian personalist ethic. Harriet was torn between these two views of women's place. She subscribed, along with her sister and many other nineteenth-century feminists, to the idea that women have a separate culture, which is more humane and morally enlightened than men's, and that they have a duty to reform the world in accordance with its tenets. This theory is called cultural feminism. On the other hand, by writing *Uncle Tom's Cabin* Stowe clearly abandoned her sister's genteel tactics—though cultural feminist doctrine is one of its central ideological assumptions.[6]

criticism

Many critics have suggested that Stowe's own experiences as wife and mother provided her with an understanding of acute oppression that translated into her depiction of slavery in the novel. A famous letter Harriet wrote in 1845 to her husband expresses her own sense of degradation. "It is a dark, sloppy, rainy, muddy, disagreeable day,"she begins. "I have been working hard . . . all day in the kitchen, washing dishes . . . seeing a great deal of that dark side of domestic life." She continues, "I am sick of the smell of sour milk, and sour meat, and sour everything, and then the clothes *will* not dry." "[M]y whole situation," she concludes, "is excessively harassing and painful." In commenting on this passage Edmund Wilson remarked that in the early years of her marriage Stowe suffered "from miseries" comparable to the "ever-rankling anxieties of slavery." Stowe herself, inadvertently perhaps, made the comparison in an 1838 letter to her friend Mary Dutton, where she explains that she views writing as her ticket to freedom: "I have about three hours per day in writing; and if you see my name coming out everywhere, you may be sure of one thing—that I do it for *the pay*. I have determined not to be a mere domestic slave."

Other critics also have suggested that Stowe herself experienced the oppression of a kind of slavery. Leslie A. Fiedler intuited that Stowe was "in her deepest self-consciousness a slave." After reading *Uncle Tom's Cabin* Charlotte Brontë suspected that Stowe herself had "felt the iron of slavery," and John R. Adams viewed the novel as Stowe's own "declaration of independence, her revolution, and her emancipation proclamation. . . . With explosive power it shrieked against the indignity of subservience."[7]

Central concern

It is also clear that Stowe's experience as a mother of seven children provided much of the novel's emotional energy, for one of its central concerns is the separation of black mothers from their children when the latter were sold. Stowe once explained that the death of her one-year-old son Charley in the 1849 cholera epidemic gave her a special empathy with slave mothers' sense of loss. "It was at his dying bed and at his grave that I learned what a poor slave mother may feel when her child is torn away from her. . . . I have often felt that much in that book ('Uncle Tom') had its root in the awful scenes and bitter sorrows of that summer."[8]

Uncle Tom's Cabin must also be seen in the context of nineteenth-century religious movements. In the most authoritative religious interpretations of the novel, Charles H. Foster and Alice Crozier identify its dominant religious ethos as Edwardsean Calvinism.[9] By this they mean it expresses the kind of Calvinism advocated by New England theologian Jonathan Edwards (1703–58).

Calvinism, one of the sects that emerged during the Protestant Reformation, early became dominant in New England. It held that God was an all-powerful, utterly unknowable, transcendent *other* whose ways were inscrutable to human beings. It also maintained that human salvation was predetermined by God (the doctrine of predestination), who selects some to be saved (the elect) by a gift of grace. The individual can do little or nothing to be saved except prepare for the reception of grace. Humans are seen as born in original sin (the doctrine of human depravity) and therefore condemned to eternal damnation unless saved.

Edwards's most famous sermon, "Sinners in the Hands of an Angry God" (1741), aptly expresses the Calvinist idea of the inscrutable deity. Even more important, however, for our purposes is his *Treatise Concerning Religious Affection* (1746), wherein he urges that "holy affections" or emotions are a "visible sign" of election. Love, he maintains, is "the fountain of all the affections."[10] This emphasis on experiential religion became the hallmark of the Great Awakening (1740–43), a revival movement led by Edwards that emphasized the importance of the inner emotional state (rather than outer social status) and therefore democratized salvation. Indeed, the principal converts during the Great Awakening were the dispossessed and powerless—women and others at the lower end of the socioeconomic scale. As Crozier and other critics have pointed out, it is clear that Stowe conceived her central characters—Tom and Eva—as those whose "holy affections" marked them as recipients of grace—members of the elect, even though socially powerless.

Stowe was also influenced by the Second Great Awakening

(1797–1831), another major revival movement, one of whose leaders was her father, Lyman Beecher. This movement picked up on another Calvinist idea—that although human society was fallen, it could be "converted" so as to conform more with God's will by activists who saw themselves as "instruments in God's plan for reordering society."[11] This premise was the catalyst for many of the social reform movements of the nineteenth century, including the temperance, abolition, and women's rights movements. Harriet Beecher Stowe strongly believed in this "social gospel"; indeed, *Uncle Tom's Cabin* has been called "the ultimate classic" of the Second Great Awakening.[12]

Finally, *Uncle Tom's Cabin* must be placed within the literary traditions of the nineteenth century. Like all great works, however, it is not just a pastiche of sources, which some critics have reduced it to, but, rather, a unique achievement that transcends its origins. Nevertheless, a number of nonfictional sources have been adduced. Stowe herself said she slept with Theodore Weld's compendium of slave reportage, *American Slavery as It Is: Testimony of a Thousand Witnesses* (1839), under her pillow while she was writing *Uncle Tom's Cabin*. It is clear that she was also familiar with a number of the "slave narratives" or autobiographies by ex-slaves that had been published by this time. In her *Key to "Uncle Tom's Cabin"* she mentions as sources narratives by Frederick Douglass and Josiah Henson and in a later letter one by Lewis Clark. Others have seen parallels between *Uncle Tom's Cabin* and the narratives by Henry Bibb, William Wells Brown, and Solomon Northrup.[13] Stowe also appears to have been familiar with earlier antislavery novels, as well as with the so-called plantation novels written by southerners, which depicted slavery in benign romantic terms.[14]

But while Stowe may have owed ideas for specific details to these sources, the overall literary shape of her work derives from the traditions of sentimentalism and realism. *Uncle Tom's Cabin* has been both dismissed and praised as an exemplum of the sentimentalist novel, a genre that was dominated by women as authors, characters, and readers. It was an enormously popular form but one that until recently critics have not taken seriously. Stowe's novel shares some sentimentalist attributes—notably an occasional tendency toward emotional hyperbole (seen especially in the Eva episodes), a Christian worldview (though *Uncle Tom's Cabin*, as we shall see, is more relentlessly Calvinist than most sentimentalist works, which generally evade the problem of evil with happy endings or otherwise simplistic solutions), and a focus on mothers and children. On the other hand, most sentimentalist novels are solipsistically concerned with one heroine whose fate depends upon securing a proper husband; marriage is therefore the desired denouement. Sentimentalist works typically evince little humor, little irony, and little realism in character, dialog, or setting (the latter is largely domestic, indoor space). In all these respects, *Uncle Tom's Cabin* does not fit the type. It does, however, express a political sensitivity to the point of view of the oppressed, which Philip Fisher has identified as a distinguishing feature of sentimentalist fiction.[15]

In other ways the novel belongs more comfortably in the tradition of realism, in particular that deriving from Irish regionalist writer Maria Edgeworth (1767–1849) and Sir Walter Scott (1771–1832), the latter of whose works Stowe was systematically rereading at the time she composed *Uncle Tom's Cabin*. Also apparent is the influence of some continental realists, in particular the Russian Nikolai Gogol (1809–52), whose *Dead Souls* (1842) bears a remarkable resemblance to *Uncle Tom's Cabin*, both in its satirical tone and its social criticism.[16]

The epic scope of Stowe's novel precludes identifying it simply as a sentimentalist work. Indeed, to my knowledge *Uncle Tom's Cabin* is the first epic novel written by a woman. The novel's panoramic sweep; its multitude of fully developed, psychologically complex, and varied characters; its realistic specificity in setting, economic milieu, environmental detail, and dialect; its bitterly sarcastic satirical tone; and Stowe's extensive use of metonymy—atypical of the sentimentalist mode—place it in the realist camp.[17]

Stowe indeed pioneered local color realism in the United States in some of her early stories, written in the 1830s. Her other major novels—*The Minister's Wooing* (1859), *The Pearl of Orr's Island* (1862), and *Oldtown Folks* (1869) (the latter an overlooked American classic)—also belong in the tradition of realism.[18]

Perhaps the best term for Stowe's prevailing stylistic mode is "creatural realism."[19] The author recognizes that worldly details and events have sacramental significance in and of themselves because the creation is blessed (here Stowe departs from orthodox Calvinism), but they also have meaning in reference to a soteriological framework—God's grand design for the world. For, in the end, unlike most realist works, *Uncle Tom's Cabin* cannot be understood without an appreciation of its profound religious and ethical grasp.

2

The Importance of the Work

Uncle Tom's Cabin is probably the most influential novel ever written, and certainly the most effective political novel (Abraham Lincoln was not being entirely facetious when he credited Stowe with having caused the Civil War). It remains the world's all-time best-seller. In the first year alone it sold 300,000 copies in the United States and a million in England. As of 1976 it had been translated into fifty-eight languages from Afrikaans to Yiddish. Nearly 150 editions, many with numerous reprints, have appeared in English. It has gone through nearly sixty editions in French (*La Case de l'oncle Tom*), over eighty in German (*Onkel Toms Hütte*), and nearly sixty in twenty-one languages of the peoples of the Soviet Union.[1]

No one disputes the novel's stature as a popular classic, and few would dispute its historical value—that it provides "a great folk picture of an age and nation."[2] In Europe it is considered "a masterpiece of social realism" on a par with the great European novels of the century.[3] But in this country its status as a literary masterpiece is still debated.

In reflecting on the question of what constitutes a "masterwork" I have concluded that we reserve the category for fiction that satisfies the following criteria: it engages in serious major or universal themes, such as how to wrest meaning from life, which ends in death and involves much apparently meaningless suffering; it develops those themes to a certain level of intelligence, sophistication, and complexity—that is, it does not provide easy answers or evasions. On the contrary, great literature expands the moral imagination. Masterpiece literature also often provides a rich variety and depth of characterization; it often presents a dense, detailed, and convincing sense of reality—whether psychological reality, an epic sense of setting, or the complexities of moral life; and finally, it must have an underlying architectonic integrity—that is, it must exhibit throughout an inherent design, or what Aristotle called *dianoia* or thought.

Uncle Tom's Cabin satisfies these criteria. First, it engages in serious, universal themes. The central issue in the novel is slavery, but Stowe clearly views slavery as a specific manifestation of the problem of evil. Therefore, while the institution of slavery has been abolished, the novel retains its relevance today because the broader issue of the existence of political evil and suffering remains. Indeed, as I shall point out below, it is because of its unflinching examination of this issue that the novel bears a haunting contemporaneity for the twentieth-century reader. It still works to enlarge our moral understanding.

Through her characters Stowe presents a series of possible responses to the moral issue of the existence of evil. George Harris, for example, a slave who escapes north, takes an essentially atheistic approach, saying that a benevolent God would not permit such atrocities as slavery to exist; Uncle Tom takes a Christian approach, that suffering is redemptive and that evil will be atoned for; the slave woman Cassy believes that violence is the only means by which evil can be vanquished; Mrs. Shelby, the Kentucky plantation mistress, and a number of Quakers who operate on the underground railway advocate nonviolent resistance and personal acts to alleviate suffering; St. Clare, a relatively benign plantation owner, counsels an apathetic stance, saying there is nothing one can do to end suffering and oppression. In short, Stowe develops a range of responses to the issue of evil, and her development of them, as we shall see, is done at a level of great moral sophistication.

Second, even a superficial reading of the novel reveals the richness and variety of Stowe's characterization. This is indeed one of her great strengths as a writer. Over a hundred characters are fully developed— from every class and from several regions, including free and slave blacks, northern and southern whites. Similarly, the epic scope of the novel, the range of its settings, and the prodigious detail of its realism provide the reader with an unrivaled sense of the texture of nineteenth-century American life.

Finally, Stowe's novel is carefully constructed according to an identifiable moral architecture. Few critics have recognized the powerful organizing design that undergirds the work. Stowe conceived *Uncle Tom's Cabin* as an *argument* against slavery; it is constructed according to a rhetorical pattern of moral antithesis. It proceeds by means of a series of antithetical characters or sets of characters, building dialectically to the climactic, allegorical final scenes in which Uncle Tom, who has assumed the status of a Christ figure, contends with Simon Legree, the Antichrist. The powerful confrontation between the two, in which Tom endures physical death but gains a spiritual triumph ("the sharp thorns became rays of glory" [554]), brings Stowe's work to an effective moral and formal resolution.

We read *Uncle Tom's Cabin* today through an overlay of twentieth-century atrocities—the Nazi concentration camps, the Soviet gulags, Hiroshima, My Lai. In an era when torture of resisting political prisoners is not uncommon, Uncle Tom's refusal to capitulate to Legree's torture as well as his refusal to engage in violence take on new meaning. One critic has suggested that he must now be seen as an existentialist hero for refusing "to acknowledge that he is a thing and . . . [for] maintain[ing] his integrity as a human being against every assault of uninhibited perverse power."[4]

Indeed, many aspects of Stowe's understanding of the dimensions of evil are strikingly modern. The novel's Calvinist deity—remote, inscrutable, wholly *other,* and silent—bears considerable resemblance to the "absent God" of the contemporary existentialist imagination. In *The Minister's Wooing* Stowe describes the relationship between humans and God as a "rungless ladder,"[5] a metaphor that rivals Kafka for the sense of absurdity and frustrated impotence it arouses. Many of the characters in *Uncle Tom's Cabin* are in a state of homelessness and exile, similar to the condition of the modern protagonist. Given Stowe's bitterly sarcastic, even cynical, tone throughout the novel, she must have intended the title somewhat ironically. Indeed, the novel has moments of Gnostic nihilism that recall its contemporary (published the preceding year), *Moby-Dick*.

Stowe recognizes the psychological destruction wrought on the human being by unremitting degradation, torture, and violence. Her descriptions of the numbed, apathetic state that slaves were reduced to, mechanisms in a relentless cycle of abuse, bear an uncanny resemblance to descriptions of concentration camp inmates during World War II.[6] Like Marxists and existentialists Stowe recognized that the root of alienation is the reduction of the person to an object, which is accomplished by torture or heavy, routinized labor. Her original subtitle for the novel was "The Man That Was a Thing," anticipating existentialist theologian Martin Buber's perception that I-it relationships are inherently evil and must be replaced by the I-thou connection.[7] Like Marxists, Stowe also saw that economic factors were a major determinant sustaining political evil.

Yet while Stowe's vision is bleakly modern in many respects, it is moderated by two factors: one, a faith in the healing powers of love and in nonviolence as a political tactic, and two, a sacramental sense of the goodness of the creation. This is where Stowe's "creatural realism" and her emphasis on the small comforts of domestic space, which some dismiss as sentimentalist fluff, take on a countervailing power. They suggest a polyvocal affirmation of this world, the "attentive love" that some have seen as the essence of the redemptive moral sensibility and the heart of great, moral literature.[8]

In her recognition that "brokenheartedness" is the net result of abuse and violence Stowe also approaches modern liberation theologies.[9] In stressing the healing powers of love as a political force—seen especially in Eva's theology and Tom's behavior—Stowe stands in the tradition of political theorists and practitioners of nonviolence that culminated in Mahatma Gandhi and Martin Luther King, Jr. The latter's theology of nonviolent resistance is inscribed in *Uncle Tom's Cabin*. It involves, King said, a "courageous confrontation of evil by the power of love, in the faith that it is better to be the recipient of violence than the inflicter of it, since the latter only multiplies the existence of violence and bitterness in the universe, while the former may develop a sense of shame in the opponent, and thereby bring about a transformation and change of heart."[10] Stowe's great character Uncle Tom exemplifies this theology.

Stowe's monumental novel retains, therefore, its relevance for the twentieth-century reader. Stowe's "shriek of moral revulsion still reaches our ears and shakes our hearts."[11]

3

Critical Reception

With the exception of a few African-American and nearly all southern estimates, the immediate critical response to *Uncle Tom's Cabin* was one of wild enthusiasm. This kind of positive appraisal continued throughout the nineteenth century. The novel fell into critical obscurity, however, for the first half of the twentieth century, and only in the past few decades have scholars and critics again begun to take it seriously.

A British critic's evaluation in 1852 typifies the tone of the earliest reviews. "To my mind it is the greatest novel ever written, and though it will seem strange, it reminded me . . . more of Shakespeare than anything modern . . . in [its] many-sidedness, and, . . . in that marvelous clearness of insight."[1] Among contemporary European writers, George Sand, George Eliot, Charlotte Brontë, Elizabeth Barrett Browning, Heinrich Heine, Charles Dickens, Ivan Turgenev, Victor Hugo, and Leo Tolstoy were all enthusiastic in their praise. Sand and Eliot thought Stowe a writer of genius, and Tolstoy saw *Uncle Tom's Cabin* as an "example of the highest art."[2]

In the United States Ralph Waldo Emerson, John Greenleaf Whittier, and James Russell Lowell were all very positive in their response. Later in the century (1868) John W. DeForest estimated it one of the great American works; an anonymous review in the *Atlanti* in 1879 called it the great American novel, an opinion ~~y~~ William Dean Howells in 1898.[3] Not surprisingly, perhaps, the southern critics' response was largely negative, and some chose to excoriate Stowe for violating their code of ladylike behavior.[4]

More interesting were the early responses by abolitionists and African-Americans. Probably the most enthusiastic of these was Frederick Douglass, a leading black abolitionist. He called *Uncle Tom's Cabin* "the *master book* of the nineteenth century" and consistently defended Stowe against attacks, expressing his own "reverence for her genius." "She who had walked, with lighted candle, through the darkest and most obscure corners of the slave's soul, and had unfolded the secrets of the slave's lacerated heart, could not be a stranger to us."[5] A similar response was issued by another ex-slave, Sella Martin, in 1867; in speaking of her difficulty in describing the horrors of being sold at the auction block, she remarked, "happily this . . . task is now unnecessary. Mrs. Stowe . . . [has] thrown sufficient light upon that horrible and inhuman agency of slavery."[6] In a later article novelist Albion W. Tourgée reported an interesting experiment he conducted after the Civil War in North Carolina. Over a period of fifteen years he asked ex-slaves to read or have read to them *Uncle Tom's Cabin* and to evaluate its accuracy with respect to slavery. In general, "they did not think of Uncle Tom as too meek, as later generations of black activists would. Instead they thought of him as unrealistically critical of his masters. Tom spoke out more frankly, the ex-slaves thought, than a real slave would have dared to."[7] Tourgée added a perceptive comment of his own—that Uncle Tom's and other slaves' propensity for debate was not characteristic. Seeing it as a New England trait, he remarked, "freedom of expression, [the] effusive interchange of ideas between master and servant . . . is quite foreign to the conditions of slavery. . . . Perhaps the most striking characteristic of slavery was the secretiveness it imposed upon the slave nature. . . . To the slave, language became in very truth an instrument for the concealment of thought, rather than its expression."[8]

The papers of the abolitionist journal, the *Liberator,* ran a lively debate on the merits of the novel soon after it was published. An unsigned article, probably by William Lloyd Garrison, praises the author for her "rare descriptive powers, a familiar acquaintance with slavery ... uncommon moral and philosophical acumen ... [and] feelings and emotions of the strongest character." It lauds the novel's endorsement of the principles of "Christian non-resistance" but wonders whether it is advocating them only for blacks and criticizes its support of colonization.[9] Henry C. Wright, a black abolitionist, criticized Tom's self-sacrificial behavior—a theme that recurs in much twentieth-century black criticism—saying that true Christianity "begets self-respect," such that it would have led Tom to take his master's "money ... horses ... clothes, or anything ... to aid him to free himself ... and [the master] from the guilt of slavery." Wright also rejected the colonization idea advocated in the novel. A refutation of Wright and defense of Stowe appeared in a later issue of the journal.[10]

Some blacks took an even stronger stand against the work. George Downing, William G. Allen, and Martin Delany were especially critical both of Tom's passivity and of the colonization scheme. The latter praised as an alternative to Tom the slave who would not submit to indignities but "would have buried the hoe deep in the master's skull."[11]

A resolution introduced by black delegates to the American and Foreign Anti-Slavery convention in New York in 1853 condemned the novel's colonization message; however, a note from Stowe read at the meeting stated she was not a colonizationist. A delegate reported that she had told him that if she were to rewrite the novel, "she would not send George Harris to Liberia."[12]

Generally, however, major black figures through the nineteenth century praised the work—mainly for its effectiveness at drawing attention to the evils of slavery. An 1853 comment by William Wells Brown, one of the first black novelists, is fairly typical. "*Uncle Tom's Cabin* has come down upon the dark abodes of slavery like a morning's sunlight ... awakening sympathy in hearts that never before felt for the slave." Black supporters of the novel included Frances E. W.

Harper, Mary Church Terrell, James Weldon Johnson, Langston Hughes, and W. E. B. Dubois.[13]

More recent black critics have been much harsher. Partly this is because, as many of them acknowledge, *Uncle Tom's Cabin* established a powerful tradition that black writers could not ignore, even if they wished to. The most strident critique came from James Baldwin in 1949. Unfortunately, while his article "Everybody's Protest Novel" has perceptive moments (he remarks that *Uncle Tom's Cabin* "is activated by . . . a theological terror"), it is marred by a misogynist and fulminating tone. Somewhat more moderate is Alex Haley's 1964 assessment, in which he acknowledges that the negative Uncle Tom stereotype stems from stage adaptations of the novel and that the current use of "Uncle Tom" as a slurring epithet is deeply ironic.[14] Black assessments retain a sense of ambivalence about the work, as do white critical assessments that focus on the question of its alleged racism.[15]

That issue is best addressed, in my view, by George M. Frederickson in *The Black Image in the White Mind* (1971). Frederickson argues that Stowe espoused the doctrine of "romantic racialism" that was popular in the nineteenth century, deriving from the cultural nationalism of German scholar Gottfried von Herder, whose idea of the *Volk* entailed a belief that ethnic groups and nations have distinctive features or attributes. Stowe clearly subscribed to this theory, not just in reference to African-Americans but also to Italians, French, and Anglo-Saxons. The particular version of romantic racialism that Stowe apparently absorbed was that developed by Alexander Kinmont, who gave a series of lectures in Cincinnati in 1837 and 1838 that Stowe undoubtedly heard or heard about. Kinmont believed that the Negro race was superior to the Caucasian and capable of developing "a great civilization" in Africa, one "far nobler" than that of whites because the latter lacked the "natural Christian" character of blacks. While these ideas may be objectionable today for their sweeping generality, they are not racist in the contemporary sense of the term, which Frederickson defines as "a belief in *de facto* Negro inferiority and opposition to black aspiration to equality."[16] In no way was Stowe racist in the latter sense; yet, as noted, she did indulge in egregious generalizations about African-Americans, generally to the effect that they were more warm-hearted, gentler, and Christian than whites.

Whether she believed these traits were innate or the product of environment and history is not entirely clear. In the section on Topsy (see further discussion in chapter 9) Stowe clearly sees character as shaped by environment, but elsewhere she is more ambiguous. Stowe's use of racial generalizations unquestionably detracts from the work; however, it does not invalidate it or mean that we should burn it. Rather, as with all past meritorious works—many of which evince similar distortions—it must be read critically and with an understanding of its historical social and ideological context.

Like most nineteenth-century women's literature *Uncle Tom's Cabin* was generally dismissed or ignored by prestigious academic critics and authors of literary histories through the first half of the twentieth century. Carl Van Doren regarded it as negligible in the *Cambridge History of American Literature* (1921), Vernon Parrington dismissed it as "noble propaganda" in *Main Currents in American Thought* (1927), E. K. Maxfield brushed it off as " 'goody goody' literature" in 1929. F. O. Mathiessen mentions *Uncle Tom's Cabin* only once briefly in his influential *American Renaissance* (1941), and by the 1950s literary histories by Arthur Hobson Quinn (1951), Marcus Cunliffe (1954), and Robert E. Spiller (1953) devote only a couple of pages each to Stowe's novel.[17]

In the 1960s, however, perhaps because of the emergence of the civil rights movement, feminism, and other radical causes, scholars and critics began to take another look at the work. What they found evoked grudging, if condescending, admiration. Leslie Fiedler discovered it to be "an astonishingly various and complex book" (1960). Edmund Wilson announced in 1962, "It is a much more impressive work than one has ever been allowed to suspect. . . . [A] critical mind is at work. . . . [It is] a whole drama of manners and morals and intellectual points of view." Like Henry James, who earlier described *Uncle Tom's Cabin* as "a wonderful 'leaping' fish," these critics seem compelled to dismiss Stowe's role in the creative process, as if they cannot bring themselves to believe a woman could have created such a great work. Edward Wagenknecht's 1965 comment is fairly typical: "Whether she completely knew it or not, Mrs. Stowe wrote *Uncle Tom's Cabin* like an artist."[18]

Other critics in the 1960s provided genuine and serious reappraisals of the work. The first and best of these was Kenneth Lynn's 1962 introduction to the Harvard reprint of the first edition. Lynn called the dismissal of *Uncle Tom's Cabin* as "good propaganda but bad art . . . one of the most unjust clichés in all of American criticism" and contended that those who so label it have simply not paid attention to its characters' complexity: "the shrewdness, the energy, the truly Balzacian variousness of Mrs. Stowe's characterizations." Comparing it to Melville's story "Benito Cerino" (1856), Lynn remarked that the latter "spins a far less complex psychological web than does *Uncle Tom's Cabin*." A few years later British writer Anthony Burgess, in a 1966 review of the Oxford edition of the novel, joined the list of begrudging encomiasts. Possibly the first to see that "structurally the book is very sound," he also noted the "remarkable roundness" of the characters. Nowadays, he said, "all we have to forgive is the style."[19]

By the 1970s and 1980s, however, thanks largely to feminist revisionary criticism, *Uncle Tom's Cabin* at last began to receive sustained serious critical attention. Indeed, it has become "a favorite text" of the New Americanist critics, an important new critical cohort.[20] Like feminist critics, the New Americanist critics are concerned with reassessing and revising the canon—that is, the accepted list of American masterworks.

Necessarily, such a reassessment raises questions about the standards by which masterworks are chosen and by whom. Most feminist and New Americanist critics feel that in the past these standards have been biased to favor works by educated white males and exclude works by women, blacks, Native Americans, and workers. In perhaps the most effective feminist challenge to the canon, "Melodramas of Beset Manhood: How Theories of American Fiction Exclude Women Authors" (1981), Nina Baym argues that American (male) critics have settled on a central masculine myth—that of the solitary male protagonist struggling against an entrammeling feminized "society"—as *the* central myth of American culture. All works that do not conform to this pattern are automatically excluded. In charting the contrasting literary fortunes of *Moby-Dick* and *Uncle Tom's Cabin*—the former ascended in critical esteem as the latter fell, Eric Sundquist notes the reason being "in part [that *Uncle Tom's Cabin*] lacks the complex philosophical intent and dense literary allusiveness of *Moby-Dick* and in part because it is in direct opposition to the rich American tradition of masculine confrontation with nature (the frontier tradition of the 'American Adam') that Melville helped to define."[21]

New Americanist and feminist critics argue, moreover, that many past critical criteria are irrelevant—especially the strictly formal aesthetic criteria devised by the New Critics in the 1940s and 1950s. Rather, they contend, political instead of aesthetic criteria should obtain. Two of the most important New Americanist revisions of *Uncle Tom's Cabin* have effectively taken this tack. Jane Tompkins and Philip Fisher urge that an essential consideration for a novel's greatness is whether it performs "cultural work"—that is, whether it effectively changes cultural ideology or the way people think about an issue. By these terms *Uncle Tom's Cabin* is, of course, one of the most important works in history.

Tompkins argues that *Uncle Tom's Cabin* must be seen in the context of the sentimentalist tradition whose Christology should be understood as a political ideology that asserts power for women. "I will argue that the work of the sentimental writers is complex and significant in ways other than those which characterize the established masterpieces. I will ask the reader to set aside some familiar categories for evaluating fiction—stylistic intricacy, psychological subtlety, epistemological complexity—and to see the sentimental novel, not as an artifice of eternity . . . but as a political enterprise . . . that both codifies and attempts to mold the values of its time."[22]

Philip Fisher provides a valuable discussion of the historical emergence of sentimentalism, seeing it as a literary expression of the political radicalism, with its concern for the oppressed, that developed in the eighteenth century. Sentimentalist works were political attempts to rouse readers' awareness and concern about oppressed groups—

22

women, children, slaves, workers, animals. Sentimentalist narrative "relates events from the point of view of the victim and is therefore a record of suffering, rather than from the point of view of the oppressor and, therefore, a record of violence." By contrast, Fisher sees the modern novel as inherently antisentimental and ironic, often presenting only the point of view of the oppressor, in a "pornography of . . . violence."[23] Hence, contemporary critics, having absorbed as a critical criterion the ironic distancing from suffering characteristic in modern fiction, find it difficult to reenter the world of the victim seen in a work like *Uncle Tom's Cabin* without ridiculing or otherwise disparaging its emotion.

Another New Americanist critic who gives *Uncle Tom's Cabin* serious attention is David S. Reynolds, but he resorts to New Critical notions when he suggests that the novel "misses literary status because its warring elements do not *fuse* to create metaphysical ambiguity or multilayered symbols, as they do in the major literature of the period." Like Ann Douglas, who presented one of the first feminist reassessments of sentimentalism, Reynolds feels that *Uncle Tom's Cabin* capitulates to a conventional sentimentalism that is not really politically subversive but rather reinforces the status quo. Lawrence Buell, on the other hand, sees the book as finally calling "for something closer to revolution than restoration" (of the people's "covenant" with God).[24]

Feminist critics have seen *Uncle Tom's Cabin* as being targeted as much against political domination by the white male and white women's concomitant impotence as against black slavery. The first to take this tack was Helen Papashvily (in 1956), who saw sentimentalist literature in general as expressing a cry of female revolt. Ellen Moers in 1977 also considered the power of the novel as stemming from the feminist anger that animated many of the great women's novels of the nineteenth century. "[B]elow the surface of the mind . . . seethed the feminine discontent that produced the literature of [women's] epic age."[25]

The first to fully recognize that *Uncle Tom's Cabin* is informed with cultural feminist ideology was Elizabeth Ammons in her important article, "Heroines in *Uncle Tom's Cabin*" (1977). Ammons says that Stowe proposes a maternal ethic as a countervalence to the dominant patriarchal ethic, which countenances such evils as slavery. Stowe "enlists the cult of motherhood" to challenge "the patriarchal status quo." Ammons urges further that the principal good characters in the novel represent "the redemptive feminine-Christ principle." Stowe saw blacks and women as linked because they had not been trained in the "masculine discipline of automatically subordinating emotion to reason, the discipline responsible in Stowe's opinion for legalized slavery." In a more recent article (1986) Jean Fagan Yellin similarly suggests that "the problem of slavery in *Uncle Tom's Cabin* [may be] finally inseparable from the issue of women's political impotence . . . [and] the hidden issue in the novel the feminist issue of political power for women." In positing "an alternative society grounded in egalitarian Christianity" and proposing "a loving maternal ethic in opposition to patriarchal values, *Uncle Tom's Cabin* endorses nineteenth-century radical ideas." Yellin, however, like Douglas and Reynolds, feels that the novel finally capitulates to a conservative ethos.[26]

Some of the most recent feminist analyses are among the most intriguing interpretations yet offered of the novel. In "Piecing and Writing" (1986) Elaine Showalter presents one of the few attempts to explain the novel's structure. She does so in "gynecritical" fashion by locating it within the context of nineteenth-century women's quilting art. The title is seen as an allusion to the popular log cabin quilt and the novel's structure as analogous to the quilt's pattern.[27]

In the first postmodernist analysis of the novel, "Changing the Letter" (1989), Hortense J. Spillers, a black feminist, criticizes Stowe for " 'orchestrat[ing]' a thematics of sacrifice as . . . a posited '*necessity*.' " In other words, she sees Stowe as having bought into a patriarchal Calvinism, which mandates that her sacrificial figures be a black man (Tom) and a sensual white female (Eva). In her most provocative interpretation Spillers sees Eva as expressing a repressed female desire, which requires her death. "Stowe's culture—its hateful fathers—has dictated here an *obedient* maternity . . . which punishes its daughters . . . for the embodiment of its own interdicted desire."[28]

Finally, Gillian Brown presents a socialist-feminist analysis in her important and stimulating article, "Getting in the Kitchen with Dinah: Domestic Politics in *Uncle Tom's Cabin*" (1984). Brown argues that Stowe's novel entails a radical critique of capitalism as well as patriarchy and that her overall design is to replace the market economy of capitalism with a planned "matriarchal domestic" economy based on "a utopian rehabilitation" of the domestic sphere. Brown argues that "Stowe's critique of American society is even more radical than Tompkins realizes, precisely because it addresses the problematic status of sentimental values noted by Douglas." In short, "Stowe calls for the reform of kitchens as a precondition to women's reform of market economy."[29]

Surprisingly, there have been no major Marxist interpretations of the novel (though Brown's article suggests a Marxist approach). Marx and Engels seem likely to have read the novel when it first appeared, and it became a favorite of the Zhdanovists in the Soviet Union, those who favored socialist realism,[30] but no sustained Marxist analysis has yet appeared in English (it has received a fair amount of critical attention in the Soviet Union, none of which has been translated).

It would seem, however, that the views of certain recent Marxist theorists would be relevant to *Uncle Tom's Cabin*, especially those of Mikhail Bakhtin, Fredric Jameson, and Ernst Bloch. Stowe's novel expresses the kind of polyphonic, dialogical mentality Bakhtin praises in *Problems of Dostoievsky's Poetics*. *Uncle Tom's Cabin* fits Bakhtin's description of a "dialogical" work. "It is not constructed as the entirety of a single consciousness which absorbs other consciousnesses as objects, but rather as the entirety of the interaction of several consciousnesses, of which no one fully becomes the object of any other one." As in Dostoievsky, the "major inspiration" of Stowe's work "is the struggle against the materialization . . . of all human values under the conditions of capitalism." In *Uncle Tom's Cabin* the central perception, similarly, is how humans may overcome reification—reduction to the status of a thing.[31]

A dialectical approach to *Uncle Tom's Cabin*, such as that theorized by Fredric Jameson, would recognize that it is an "allegory of desire." Jameson sees that the author is a politically situated being and that creativity involves the creation of "imaginary or 'formal' solutions to unresolveable social contradictions." It is Ernst Bloch who has most stressed this utopian dimension of imaginative literature. According to Bloch, all great art expresses a dialectical critique of social evil, providing an "anticipatory illumination" of alternative arrangements. In his collection *Marxism and Art* Maynard Solomon explains that Marx and Engels's vision of a classless society is really that of a "primitive matriarchal communism."[32] Harriet Beecher Stowe's utopian vision in *Uncle Tom's Cabin*, as well as in her other major works, is of such a world.

A Reading

4

Style, Structure, and Themes: The Problem of Evil

In the 1889 authorized biography of Harriet Beecher Stowe, written with her blessing and collaboration, the author, her son Charles, says that in writing *Uncle Tom's Cabin* Stowe "no more thought of style or literary excellence than the Mother who rushes into the street and cries for help to save her children from a burning house thinks of the rhetorician or the elocutionist."[1] Assuming that this statement comes from Stowe herself, it is somewhat disingenuous, as are others of its ilk she made throughout her career. Contrary to the impression it gives, Stowe was hardly a naive illiterate who could barely string words together. Instead, she was highly trained in rhetoric and dialectical thinking; indeed she taught rhetoric at the Hartford Female Seminary for several years. In an 1830 letter Stowe comments on how she has been practicing Johnsonian rhetoric: "Have been reading Raselas [sic] and writing a little in imitation of Dr. Johnson's style—think it is improving me by giving me a command of language. . . . For half an afternoon I . . . could not even shut a closet door except in a double antithesis."[2]

Stowe's decision to use an informal, unpolished style in *Uncle Tom's Cabin* was a deliberate one. It was designed to make the work accessible to the common reader. Stowe's overriding purpose in writing the novel was to *persuade* her audience that slavery was intolerable. To do this she could not risk alienating it with what she later called "the 'hifalutin' style"—precious diction, latinate constructions, and circumlocution. Rather she chose the "plain style" of the Puritan rhetorical tradition, modified by the conversational easiness characteristic of the "dashaway or familiar" style of the women's epistolary tradition.[3] Stowe establishes an intimacy with the reader by regular use of "we"—author and reader together—and by directly addressing the reader, whom she usually sees as a white mother like herself.[4] Most of the narrative in *Uncle Tom's Cabin* is direct discourse, dialog between characters, often heated intellectual discussions and debate. This stylistic feature further heightens the novel's sense of immediacy.

Stowe conceived of her work as a series of dramatized scenes. She explained her concept to Gamaliel Bailey, editor of the *National Era*, where the work first appeared in serial form. It was to be "a series of sketches," she explained. "My vocation is simply that of a painter. . . . There is no arguing with *pictures*" (letter of 9 March 1851). Later she said she arranged the incidents in *Uncle Tom's Cabin* "in the same manner that the mosaic artist groups . . . fragments of various stones into one general picture."[5]

The latter comment suggests the patchwork composition Elaine Showalter noted as a structural feature. Certainly, Stowe's surface style is paratactic—that of a "verbal quilt" where pieces or scenes are simply placed side by side and joined without subordination.[6] Stowe's juxtapositions are usually done, however, for both ironic and aesthetic effect; that is, events are set side by side so as to comment silently on one another, as in the unspoken irony of the slave narratives. Or they may be juxtaposed to change the mood or aesthetic effect: dark, somber scenes are often followed by light, comic episodes.

But the patchwork quilt analogy is finally too static to adequately encompass the powerful dynamic of Stowe's novel. *Uncle Tom's Cabin* is a work of movement; its organizing design is dialectical; its pattern a powerful process of transformations.

These transformations occur primarily in space rather than time (the novel covers approximately five years, but Stowe is vague about temporal transitions). As Philip Fisher perceptively observes, events in *Uncle Tom's Cabin* happen suddenly, which contributes to the sense of a spatial rather than a temporal dynamic. Fisher suggests that the suddenness of occurrences reflects the point of view of the oppressed. Little causal or temporal subordination is provided, for that would provide rationalization for the act, the viewpoint of the oppressor.

> Sentimental narrative avoids the roots of actions in the past . . . because all of our interest in these antecedents is aimed at understanding why the act occurred. It is made more reasonable and acceptable. . . . [and] we identify with the actor rather than the victim, because, for the victim such acts are unexpected. . . . Only for the oppressor do such acts have a past. To give the narration a past is to recognize or implicitly adopt the point of view of the oppressor. In *Uncle Tom's Cabin* all the essential events occur suddenly. The novel begins with the slave buyer already signing the purchase for Uncle Tom. . . . By this means Stowe avoids interest in the motives or psychology of the oppressor.[7]

Not only events but characters are introduced suddenly, encountered as if at random because they are geographically there when a central character arrives on the scene. One of Stowe's most daring narrative feats is to introduce several of her major characters late in the work. But neither events nor characters are really appearing at random, of course. Rather they are part of Stowe's dialectical design, which shaped her arrangement of elements.

Stowe early received rigorous training in dialectical thinking. At the age of twelve she presented a composition, "Can the Immortality of the Soul Be Proved by the Light of Nature?"—a work of several pages—that is remarkable for its dialectical organization. A similar structure underlies *Uncle Tom's Cabin*. It is arranged according to the rhetorical principle of antithesis.

Characters and sets of characters and events are set in opposition to one another. The novel progresses from thesis to antithesis or by means of the growth of an antithetical principle out of its opposite.

The landscape of *Uncle Tom's Cabin* is a moral geography. The map of America becomes a symbolic realm, ranged according to moral antipodes: to the north lies the good; to the south, evil. The two principal plots in the work—the passage of Uncle Tom south and the Harris family north—are not disconnected, as some commentators have charged, but rather held in dialectical counterpoint.

The novel, in fact, is symmetrically organized. Approximately eleven chapters take place in relatively benign, comfortable domestic spaces in the border states or the North, approximately eleven chapters concern people in transit—in taverns, on boats, in slave auctions, etc. Twelve chapters cover the events at the St. Clare estate, and nine, at the Legree plantation.

Moreover, the geography of *Uncle Tom's Cabin* registers a symbolic spectrum: from north to south, as noted, and from good to evil; but also from cool to hot; from order to disorder; from reason to the irrational; from sacred to profane; from active to passive; from agent to victim; from egalitarian to master-slave relationships; from planned economies (socialist kitchens) based on use-value production, where people are treated with dignity and the primary concern is with human welfare, to unbridled capitalism where people are treated as commodities and the primary motive is profit; from a world of plenty to one of deprivation.

The principal characters' movement follows these loci. Uncle Tom leaves the benign, middle ground of Kentucky in early spring, where he has had a modicum of active control over his life; it is cool; life is orderly. He moves to the South where experience is increasingly hotter, disordered, irrational, and evil, where his destiny is passive objectification. The nadir, the hell, of the novel is Legree's plantation, which is intensely hot, disorderly, irrational, and profoundly evil. An alternative further north is the Quaker kitchen in Ohio, which is cool, ordered, rational, and benignly egalitarian. Canada and Stowe's utopian notion of Africa represent the positive end of the spectrum.

The fundamental ritual behind these dialectical transitions is the one that underlies classical tragedy as well as Christian theology—the vegetative passage of the year, from life to death and death to life, expressed symbolically in the Christian resurrection myth. Thus, after the suffering and death of Tom follow the happy, resurrectory scenes of the Harrises in Canada on their way to a utopian future. In the conception of its moral geography, if not in its structure (Dante began his work with *Inferno*, but Stowe ends there), *Uncle Tom's Cabin* bears a resemblance to the *Divine Comedy*. Tom and Eva's beatific visions of the afterlife and Stowe's utopian dream of Africa suggest the *Paradiso*, whereas the middle areas of Kentucky and the St. Clare estate recall the *Purgatorio*.

The principal theme in *Uncle Tom's Cabin* is the problem of evil. Stowe handles the issue on several levels: theological, moral, economic, political, and practical.

The theological dimension of the problem is raised early in the novel through the character George Harris, a slave whose pet dog has been killed by his master and who has been whipped for refusing to obey orders to kill the dog himself. As George vows vengeance, his wife, Eliza, cautions him against it, urging a Christian solution—to have faith in God's ultimate judgment. George counters by posing the basic question of the problem of evil: why does an allegedly just deity allow it to exist? "I ain't a Christian like you Eliza," he says; "my heart's full of bitterness; I can't trust in God. Why does he let things be so?" (62).

Later, in recounting how his sister has been sold into sexual slavery, George suggests an even grimmer, Gnostic possibility—that the gods themselves are evil powers, supporting the forces of evil. "Is God on their side?" George asks. If not, he repeats, "Why does he let such things happen?" (290). At this point in the novel Stowe again counterposes to George the idea of faith in a just, retributive God, here provided by the Quaker Simeon, who reads from Psalm 73.

Immediately following this intellectual exchange Stowe presents an example of a small act of charity that serves both to comment ironically on the weighty preceding discussion, because it is a gratuitous act of goodness, and to exemplify one of Stowe's major responses to the question of evil—that it can be countered effectively by individual acts of kindness. In this instance Rachel, a Quaker woman in whose home George, Eliza, and their son have found refuge, takes Eliza's hand and leads her to the dinner table. Just then Ruth, another Quaker, rushes in with some woolen stockings and a seed-cake for Harry, the boy. It should be mentioned as well that these Quakers are engaging in civil disobedience; by taking in escaped slaves, they are in violation of the 1850 Fugitive Slave Law and could serve time in prison if they are discovered. This scene exemplifies one of Stowe's central political and practical responses to the specific evil slavery; namely, her endorsement of nonviolent resistance to the law.

The theological issue of God's silence in the face of atrocious evil is also raised early in the novel. An authorial comment made in connection with the forceful separation of a black wife from her husband again counsels faith but acknowledges doubt. These stories of suffering, Stowe urges, are being heard "in the ear of One who is not deaf, though he be long silent" (202).

Augustine St. Clare, the Louisiana slaveholder who buys Tom but who dislikes the system of slavery, presents an apathetic position on the question of evil. In being challenged for his complaisant acquiescence to an evil system by his northern cousin Ophelia, St. Claire responds: "here is a whole class,—debased, uneducated, indolent, provoking,—put, without any sort of terms or conditions, entirely into the hands of such people as the majority in our world are; people who have neither consideration nor self-control. . . . [W]hat can a man of honorable and humane feelings do, but shut his eyes all he can, and harden his heart? I can't buy every poor wretch I see. I can't turn knight-errant, and undertake to redress every individual case of wrong. . . . The most I can do is to try and keep out of the way of it" (328).

Later, shaken by his daughter Eva's death, St. Clare questions Uncle Tom about his faith and thereby about his belief in an ultimate redemption of suffering and death—another approach to the problem of evil. "How do you know there's any Christ, Tom! You never saw the Lord." Tom's answer is that of Edwardsean Calvinism: "Feel Him in my Soul, Mas'r" (436). Tom suggests that he read the New Testament Gospel of John, chapter 11, which treats the raising of Lazarus from the dead. In it Jesus says, "I am the resurrection, and the life. . . . And whosoever liveth and believeth in me shall never die" (John 11:25–26). St. Clare observes in surprise of Tom, "This is all *real* to you!" But he challenges Tom with his own agnosticism. "Tom, you know that I have a great deal more knowledge than you; what if I should tell you that I don't believe this Bible? . . . Wouldn't it shake your faith some . . . ?" (437). Tom again speaks from an Edwardsean position, saying the Lord "hides from the wise and prudent, and reveals unto babes" (437), thereby establishing the superiority of his own intuitive religious faith to the enlightened skepticism of St. Clare.

St. Clare himself, however, becomes increasingly morbid and moodily reflective. He comes to sense the possibility of divine retribution and comes to feel that apathetic good people like himself will be swept away by God's wrath as soon as those more actively evil. Tom provides him with the relevant scriptural passage, Matthew 26:34–40: Those will be "cursed . . . into everlasting fire" who failed to give solace to the suffering. When St. Clare asks whether Tom thinks this applies to his master, Tom does not answer. Shortly thereafter St. Clare begins playing the "Dies Irae" of Mozart's *Requiem Mass* on the piano, suggesting an acceptance of the idea of the last judgment (449–50). After St. Clare's death, however, and as the world of the novel darkens, Stowe's conviction of the existence of a just God seems to be shaken. The sheer contingency of the slave Emmeline, on the eve of a slave auction—her and her mother's horrible dependency—make their reliance on prayer seem especially pathetic. Surely Stowe is entertaining the possibility of the futility of prayer when she reassures that "God has not forgotten" the many such prayers that have already "gone up from these same . . . slave-prisons" (473). Later, on hearing the sorrowful story of another slave woman, Emmeline's faith is further tried. Stowe asks, "Would it not try the faith of the firmest Christian, to find themselves abandoned, apparently, of God, in the grip of ruthless violence?" (487).

On Legree's plantation Stowe raises the possibility that God simply does not exist in the depths of evil. God only looks down "calm and

silent . . . on the scene of misery and oppression. . . . 'Is God HERE?' "
(497). Cassy, a much-abused slave woman, says no. "There's no use
calling on the Lord . . . he never hears . . . there isn't any God, I believe;
or, if there is, he's taken sides against us. All goes against us, heaven and
earth. Everything is pushing us into hell. Why shouldn't we go?" (512).
Cassy's position, an extension of George Harris's, is perhaps the most
nihilistic and, sadly, the most modern, in the novel. Even Tom comes to
have doubts in this cesspool of unremitting affliction. "O Jesus!" he
cries out, "have you quite forgot us poor critturs?" (513). Cassy says the
other slaves on the plantation, long abused and degraded, have lost their
sense of humanity and any hope of deliverance—whether religious or
political. "We live in filth and grow loathsome, till we loathe ourselves!
And we long to die, and we don't dare to kill ourselves!—No hope! no
hope! no hope?" (515). After he has been tortured, Tom too finds his
faith shaken. "The gloomiest problem of this mysterious life was constantly before his eyes,—souls crushed and ruined, evil triumphant, and
God silent" (552).

On the moral level, Stowe evinces the modern existentialist awareness that evil manifests itself in the objectification of human beings,
their transformation into commodities or things for economic use.
Marxists use the term *reification,* which is based on the Latin word
res, or *thing,* to identify the process by which workers become
commodified as objects in factory labor. Stowe saw similarly that in
the system of slavery human beings were seen as soulless objects, mere
property, to be disposed of as the owner wished. Her recognition that
the phenomenon of objectification was at the heart of slavery's evil
may be seen in the novel's original subtitle—"The Man That Was a
Thing."

The novel's most bitingly ironic comments on the commodification of people come in sections where slave traders are discussing their
"wares." The slave trader Haley explains to Mr. Shelby, the Kentucky
plantation owner who sells him Tom, that he finds it good business to
treat slaves humanely. Rough treatment "damages the article," which
depreciates their value (47). Other attributes, conversely, increase the
"article's" value. Religion, for example, is "a valeyable thing in a

nigger" because it makes the slave compliant, Haley remarks—thus commodifying a person's spirituality as a commercial extra, like air conditioning or an FM radio in a car.

Later in the novel St. Clare parodies the slave traders' appraisal of their "goods" by estimating his own value—an example of Stowe's use of comic inversion. "I wonder, now," he reflects, "if I was divided up and inventoried . . . how much I might bring. Say so much for the shape of my head, so much for a high forehead, so much for arms, and hands, and legs, and then so much for education, learning, talent, honesty, religion!" (237).

More seriously, Stowe examines the sexual commodification of black women. In the opening scene Haley instinctively appraises Eliza's sexual attractiveness and offers to buy her knowing she will bring a good price as a prostitute: "a delicately formed hand and a trim foot and ankle were items of appearance that did not escape the quick eye of the trader, well used to run up at a glance the points of a fine female article" (45). Later, when Emmeline is being prepared for sale, the trader tells her to curl her hair: "Them curls may make a hundred dollars difference in the sale of her" (475). And when she was put on the market Cassy found, "they made me dress up, every day; and gentlemen used to come in and stand and smoke their cigars, and look at me, and ask questions, and debate my price" (520).

Here, as elsewhere, Stowe's principal ironic vehicle is the insistence that these "objects" are subjects who see and understand what is happening to them. Two of her chapter titles, 10 and 11—"The Property Is Carried Off" and "In Which Property Gets into an Improper State of Mind"—highlight this irony. After a slave auction "the article enumerated as 'John, aged thirty' " speaks to Tom, explaining that he has a wife. Shortly thereafter the woman appears at the riverboat where the "merchandise" is being transported: she "flew up to where the slave gang sat, and threw her arms round that unfortunate piece of merchandise before enumerated—'John aged thirty,' and with sobs and tears bemoaned him as her husband" (202). Later Stowe remarks how slaves can be sold as chairs or tables that may once have "decorated the superb saloon" only to end up in "the bar-room of some filthy tavern. . . . The great difference," however, she observes is "that the table and chair cannot feel, and the *man* can" (481). One of the reasons Stowe belabored this point is that a principal defense of slavery—astonishing as it may seem today—was the argument that blacks do not feel or think like whites and therefore are not as sensitive to pain and suffering.[8] "These critters ain't like white folks, you know," Haley remarks; "they gets over things" (47). Here he is referring to slave mothers' loss of their children. Later, Eva counters this theory, in one of the principal arguments against slavery she makes to her father, St. Clare: "Papa, these poor creatures love their children as much as you do me" (403). Eva, in fact, contends that blacks have immortal souls and are thus equal to whites before God (410, 415).

Yet they are not equal before the law, and this injustice is a further aspect of slaves' reification that Stowe decries. On the riverboat Tom watches the agony of the slave Lucy, whose child has just been sold from her. Here Stowe casts the evil in terms of legal commodification. "His very soul bled within him for what seemed to him the *wrongs* of the poor suffering thing that lay like a crushed reed on the boxes; the feeling, living, bleeding, yet immortal *thing*, which American law coolly classes with the bundles, and bales, and boxes, among which she is lying" (210) (Stowe's emphasis). "The law regards [the slave], in every respect, as devoid of rights as a bale of merchandise" (457).

Earlier, in criticizing his owner's deplorable treatment of George Harris, Stowe remarks "as this young man was in the eye of the law not a man, but a thing, all [his] superior qualifications were subject to the control of a vulgar, narrow-minded, tyrannical master" (55). Nevertheless, George's inner feelings betray that he is a feeling, thinking human being: "the flashing eye, the gloomy and troubled brow, were part of a natural language that could not be repressed,—indubitable signs, which showed too plainly that the man could not become a thing" (56).

Other aspects of slaves' objectification are examined by Stowe. Whites' condescension is shown without comment; often young slaves are treated as pet animals and asked to perform tricks (44, 352, 369).

Mrs. Shelby sees her slaves as children (83, 98). Tom's masters refer to him as "boy" (112, 238, 256).

Stowe shows further the brutalizing effect the system has on the slaves psychologically, how they become dissociated from themselves by donning masks to please the master, a characteristic schizophrenia seen in oppressed groups, as contemporary theorists such as Frantz Fanon have pointed out.[9]

> The dealers in the human article make scrupulous and systematic efforts to promote noisy mirth among [the slaves], as a means of drowning reflection, and rendering them insensible to their condition. The whole object of the training to which the negro is put . . . is systematically directed toward making him callous, unthinking, and brutal. . . . [In the slave warehouse, where the slaves await auction] a fiddle is kept commonly going among them, and they are made to dance daily. . . . Briskness, alertness, and cheerfulness of appearance, especially before observers, are constantly enforced upon them, both by the hope of thereby getting a good master, and the fear of all that the driver may bring upon them if they prove unsalable. (468–69)

But the ultimate destruction of the human personality occurs as a result of the heavy, alienated labor the slaves must perform at the Legree plantation. "From the earliest dawn of the day, they had been in the fields, pressed to work under the driving lash of the overseers. . . . [T]he worst torture of the inquisition is produced by drop after drop, drop after drop, falling . . . with monotonous succession, on the same spot; and work, in itself not hard, becomes so, by being pressed hour after hour, with unvarying, unrelenting sameness, with not even the consciousness of free-will to take from its tediousness" (495). In looking on the slave gang of cotton workers Tom "saw only sullen, scowling, imbruted men, and feeble, discouraged women, or women that were not women,—the strong pushing away the weak . . . ; and who, treated in every way like brutes, had sunk as nearly to their level as it is possible for human beings to do" (495).

5

Themes Continued:
Responses to Evil

Stowe's principal assumption in *Uncle Tom's Cabin* is that the roots of evil are economic. Most wrongdoing and evil behavior in the novel are shown to have monetary motives. In this Stowe links slavery with capitalism, and her critique of the profit motive therefore remains relevant today. The precipitating events of the novel—the sale of Uncle Tom and attempted sale of Eliza's son Harry—happen because Mr. Shelby, Tom and Eliza's owner, is in debt. Although basically a benign person, he is forced into an evil transaction for financial reasons. He has gone into debt through unwise speculation (playing on the capitalist market), and if his mortgage is revoked, he will be forced to sell all his slaves, along with the rest of his property (43, 51, 84). Shelby, thus, is not directly speculating with his slaves, but Stowe remarks that others, particularly in the deep South, are rendered callously hard-hearted by "the prospect of sudden and rapid gain . . . with no heavier counterpoise than the interests of the helpless and unprotected" (50).

Mrs. Shelby's personalist ethic, which values personal connection over profit, is counterposed to her husband's economic motivation, but her own ignorance of economic affairs and impotence before her husband's power render her protest against the sale of Tom and Harry largely ineffective (she does manage to help Eliza escape, however). She tells Shelby that she is willing to "make a pecuniary sacrifice" in order to prevent the slaves' sale, which she condemns as an "open acknowledgment that we care for no tie, no duty, no relation, however sacred, compared with money" (83).

Other ugly events are seen to have economic causes. The death of George's dog is required because his master thinks it costs too much to feed him (62). Cassy's white lover/owner betrays her because he can see no way of paying off his debts except by selling her (518). One of the bitterest incidents in the novel occurs in a Kentucky slave auction where an older slave woman, partially blind and crippled, is hoping to be sold together as a package deal with her only remaining son, fourteen-year-old Albert. The woman resorts to selling herself to slave traders before the auction, stressing, "I can cook yet, and scrub, and scour,—I'm wuth a buying, if I do come cheap" (195). Haley, however, who buys the boy, refuses to purchase her as well, basing his decision on economic calculations: "Why, she's an old rack o'bones,—not worth her salt. . . . half blind, crooked with rheumatis, and foolish to boot" (195). In a later episode an absentee northerner ("a member of a Christian church in New York" [471]), who has inherited a plantation, has to sell it and its slaves to avoid bankruptcy. "He didn't like trading in slaves and souls of men,—of course, he didn't; but, then, there were thirty thousand dollars in the case, and that was rather too much money to be lost for a principle" (472).

St. Clare, the philosopher of the novel, presents a theory of economic determinism that is essentially Marxist (some of his other ideas are also Marxist, as we shall see). In underscoring her economic thesis throughout the novel, Stowe seems to endorse St. Clare's theory. In a discussion with his wife, Marie, and cousin Ophelia, St. Clare dismisses the idea that scripture provides justification for slavery. Scripture, he says, is read in accordance with the economic necessities of the day—an idea formulated by Marx as follows: "The mode of production of material life conditions the social, political, and intellectual life process in general."[1]

St. Clare continues, were economic realities to change, the reading of scripture would change accordingly: "[S]uppose that something should bring down the price of cotton once and forever, and make the whole slave property a drug in the market, don't you think we should soon have another version of the Scripture doctrine?" (281). In other words, the Bible may be used to support slavery when it is profitable, but if it were to become unprofitable, scripture would be read to support its abolition. In short, ideology follows material interest, a central Marxist tenet.

As might be expected, the most egregious example of uncontrolled capitalism is to be found at the plantation of Simon Legree. Stowe considers that a principal factor in Legree's pathology is his capitalist mentality; he "used [his property], as he did everything else, merely as an implement for money-making" (491). Thus, Legree exploits the plantation hands as mere mechanisms in his cotton-picking factory, running through them as one would replaceable parts. His philosophy is: "I don't go for savin' niggers. Use up, and buy more, 's my way;—makes you less trouble, and I'm sure it comes cheaper in the end" (485). When asked how long the slaves last at this kind of brutal labor, he replies:

> Well, dunno; 'cordin' as their constitution is. Stout fellers last six or seven years; trashy ones gets worked up in two or three. I used to, when I first begun, have considerable trouble fussin' with 'em and trying to make 'em hold out,—doctorin' on 'em up when they's sick, and givin' on 'em clothes and blankets, and what not, tryin' to keep 'em all sort o' decent and comfortable. Law, 't wasn't no sort o' use. I lost money on 'em, and 't was heaps o' trouble. Now, you see, I just put 'em straight through, sick or well. When one nigger's dead, I buy another, and I find it comes cheaper and easier, every way. (485)

The ideology that Stowe counterposes to the unbridled amoral capitalism of the Legree plantation and of slavery in general is an amalgam of cultural feminism, Edwardsean Calvinism, and the Quaker philosophy of the "living Gospel" and nonviolent resistance.

Many critics have noted the cultural feminist aspect of *Uncle*

Tom's Cabin—the idea that white women, especially mothers, have a more personalist, humane ethic than white men and that it provides both a position from which to criticize patriarchal politics and a model on which to base an alternative world. In general, Stowe believed that these women—along with most blacks and children—have an immediate, emotional revulsion to evil. Largely, she felt, this was because they have not been educated in abstract, rationalizing systems that obfuscate personal responses to individual instances of suffering and pain. In a later novel, *The Minister's Wooing* (1859), Stowe wrote, "where theorists and philosophers tread with sublime assurance, woman often follows with bleeding footsteps; women are always turning from the abstract to the individual, and feeling where the philosopher only thinks."[2]

In *Uncle Tom's Cabin* Stowe dramatizes numerous examples of the confrontation between men's tendency toward abstract rationalization and women's toward compassionate concern about individual cases. (Indeed, one of Stowe's major reasons for writing the novel was based on the assumption that [primarily women] readers would be more moved to oppose slavery by an array of dramatized individual instances of cruelty than by abstract arguments.)

St. Clare, for example, remarks how his mother had to petition his slaveholding father: "I used sometimes to hear my mother reasoning cases with him,—endeavoring to excite his sympathies. He would listen to the most pathetic appeals with the most discouraging politeness and equanimity," dismissing her pleas with the comment "General rules will bear hard on particular cases" (336–37).

In *The Key to "Uncle Tom's Cabin"* Stowe excoriates abstract legalistic discussions of slavery that ignore the reality of individuals' suffering. She compares such "legal *nonchalence*" to "running a dissecting-knife through the course of all the heartstrings of a living subject, for the purpose of demonstrating the laws of nervous contraction."[3] In *Uncle Tom's Cabin* perhaps the most dramatic confrontation between "heartless" male abstractions and a female ethic of the heart occurs in the debate between Senator and Mrs. Bird.

As a member of the U.S. Senate, Bird voted for the Fugitive Slave

Law. But Mrs. Bird, whose ethical sensitivity is such that "anything in the shape of cruelty would throw her into a passion" (143), says she will break that law the first chance she has (144). He condescendingly tells her one must suppress one's private feelings in order to support the "public interest"—thus allowing a general abstraction to erase an immediate emotional response. "We mustn't suffer our feelings to run away with our judgment; you must consider it's a matter of private feeling,—there are great public interests involved" (144). He says he can present an array of arguments in favor of the law; to which she responds, "O, nonsense, John!—you can talk all night, but . . . would *you* now turn away a poor, shivering, hungry creature . . . because he is a runaway?" (145). He argues that it would be his "duty," which she roundly rejects. "[L]et me reason with you," he says. She exclaims, "I hate reasoning" because it is usually a form of casuistry that ignores morality (145).

At this point Eliza, a fugitive slave, arrives at their door so the issue is no longer hypothetical. Finally, under Mrs. Bird's influence, the senator agrees to help Eliza and her son escape, thus committing civil disobedience. Mrs. Bird praises him, saying, "Your heart is better than your head, in this case" (153). Stowe comments ironically how "the real presence of distress" had forced the senator to recant his support of an abstract law. "He had never thought that a fugitive might be a hapless mother, a defenceless child" (156). Thus, confrontation with an individual case of suffering breaks through abstractions (such as the law) that would elide its existence.

Many white women act on their principles to subvert the system; both Mrs. Shelby and Mrs. Bird commit civil disobedience in helping Eliza and Harry to escape. Mrs. Shelby shows genuine empathy for Aunt Chloe, Uncle Tom's wife, and helps her at critical points in the narrative, and Eva establishes a healing relationship with Topsy. On the other hand, Marie St. Clare is an egregiously selfish and heartless white woman, and several white men are compassionate and help fugitives escape—for example, John Van Trompe, a former Kentucky slave owner who had freed his slaves and become an operative on the underground railway (159); and Simeon Halliday and Phineas Fletcher, Quakers who regularly risk imprisonment for helping fugitive slaves escape north. So, Stowe's division of humane attributes along gender lines is not absolute.

It is clear, however, that the domestic world, when run properly in accordance with a Christian ethic, is Stowe's political model for how society at large should operate. In particular, the home of the Quaker family, the Hallidays, seems to provide a utopian glimpse of the perfect society: it is egalitarian, orderly, and infused with "an atmosphere of mutual confidence and good fellowship" (223). The dominating presence is the mother, Rachel. "There was so much motherliness and fullheartedness even in the way she passed a plate of cakes or poured a cup of coffee, that it seemed to put a spirit into the food and drink she offered" (223). Here one discovers "a living Gospel, breathed in living faces, preached by a thousand unconscious acts of love and good will" (224). (The same kind of atmosphere pervades Uncle Tom and Aunt Chloe's home, the cabin of the title, but it is darkened by the reality of slavery.)

I think Stowe's ultimate solution to the problem of slavery and to the problem of evil lies in these scenes. Although she considers the eventuality of an apocalyptic last judgment (indeed the final lines of the work prophesy the "wrath of Almighty God!" [629]), and she entertains the possibility of a violent slave rebellion (299, 344, 391–92) and considers colonization as a postabolition alternative, her ultimate solution demands a moral revolution.

Stowe's use of the metaphor of the heart throughout helps us to understand the nature of this revolution: it requires a mass *change of heart* (*metanoia* or conversion). What is needed, Stowe believed, to counter the reign of evil, with its objectification of the person and destruction of the personality—"brokenheartedness"—is the "fullheartedness" that animates the Halliday home. Such an attitude is described by contemporary Christian philosopher Simone Weil in the following terms: "The love of our neighbor in all its fullness simply means being able to say . . . 'What are you going through?' "[4] Were slaveholders and traders, politicians and lawyers, to allow themselves this kind of charitable awareness, slavery and a host of other evils would simply cease to exist because the rationalizations that legitimate them—whether they be economic, legal, or religious—would be overcome.

To an extent Stowe derived this idea of a mass emotional conversion from Edwardsean Calvinism. Tom and Eva are clearly Edwardsean characters, elect by the fullness of their loving hearts. Stowe, however, seems to be moving away from the arbitrariness of orthodox Calvinism and toward a religion in which people can choose the path of salvation (now conceived primarily in terms of this world) by electing a change of heart within themselves and choosing to operate according to an ethic of caring and compassion—the living Gospel. In other words, Stowe is moving toward a religion of salvation by works rather than by grace. The works philosophy predominates in her later novels.

In *Uncle Tom's Cabin* it is Uncle Tom and Eva who exemplify Stowe's religion of love. In keeping with Stowe's ethic of immediacy, Tom does not allow abstract generalizations to obscure the reality of individual instances of evil. Stowe comments sarcastically: "To him, it looked like something unutterably horrible and cruel, because, poor ignorant black soul! he had not learned to generalize, and to take enlarged views" (209). Similarly Tom's understanding of religion is not obscured by pedantic scholarship; he does not "fill his head first with a thousand questions of authenticity of manuscript, and correctness of translation" (229). In other words, Tom's religion is not intellectually based; rather it is an intuitive religion of the heart. Tom's refusal to retaliate violently against the torture meted out by Legree is rooted in his belief in the redemptive powers of love and in his understanding that violence reduces a person to a thing, a process that can intensify to the point where one is no longer human and therefore no longer saveable. Tom is one of those who, in the words of Jean-Paul Sartre, "broke the circle of Evil and reaffirmed the human—for themselves, for us, and for their very tormentors."[5]

Eva—like Tom acivilized in that she is female and too young to have been educated in the ways of patriarchal civilization—also expresses an intuitive experiential religion. Stowe continually emphasizes how instances of suffering and evil afflict her personally, using once again the heart metaphor. "These things sink into my heart," she tells Tom, after hearing the slave Prue's searing story (326). After listening to a similar story later, "the child's small frame trembled and shook with the violence of her feelings." Again she explains, this time to her father, "These things *sink into my heart*" (347; Stowe's emphasis). Indeed, one senses that Eva's mysterious illness is a result of her capacity to absorb the suffering of others to the point of excruciation.

Love proves redemptive for two of the most abused and alienated characters in the novel, Topsy and Cassy. As Tom remarks, a religion of love can "bind up the brokenhearted" (556), a phrase repeated by Mrs. Shelby as she consoles Aunt Chloe on the death of Tom (615). This is the ultimate message of the novel, expressed most graphically in Eva's dying address to the slaves in which she simply says "I love you" (418). Fittingly, these were Stowe's own dying words (said to her nurse).

6

The Cabin and the Plantation

Uncle Tom's Cabin can be roughly divided into three sections. The first covers the episodes in Kentucky and Ohio—the middle ground—where Tom is sold and begins his journey south and Eliza and George escape and begin their itinerary north. The second covers Tom's trip down the Mississippi River and his stay at the St. Clare estate in Louisiana, and the third includes the events at the Legree plantation and George and Eliza's arrival in Canada.

The title of the first chapter, "In Which the Reader Is Introduced to a Man of Humanity," sets the ironic tone for the opening episodes of the novel. "Man of Humanity" is intended as an ironic epithet for Mr. Haley, the slavetrader who purchases the slaves Tom and Harry from Mr. Shelby in the opening scene. Haley explains to Shelby that it is good business to be humane, thus commodifying the attribute as commercially expedient.

As throughout the novel, the opening sections are based on the principle of antithesis. Two great but antithetical worlds are set side by side: the world of the dominant whites, the Shelby plantation, and the world of the oppressed blacks, the cabin of Uncle Tom and Aunt Chloe. The irony that operates here, as throughout, is provided by having the point of view of the oppressed comment critically on the attitudes and behavior of the oppressors. The opening dialog between Haley and Shelby is partially overheard by Eliza, the slave whose son Harry is to be part of the sale. Her point of view provides the ironic counterpoint: she sees the sale as a *subject,* where the slave traders are seeing her and her relations as *objects.*

Another aspect of Stowe's style is apparent on the first page— namely, her tendency to see characters as representative types. As noted earlier, this is a feature of Menippean satire, a generic attribute of many realistic novels (see chap. 1, n. 17). Haley is described as being a variant of the "species" *gentlemen.* In fact, the metonymic details of Stowe's description make it clear that he is a nouveau riche would-be gentleman.

> He was a short, thick-set man, with coarse, commonplace features, and that swaggering air of pretension which marks a low man who is trying to elbow his way upward in the world. He was much over-dressed, in a gaudy vest of many colors, a blue neckerchief, bedropped gaily with yellow spots, and arranged with a flaunting tie, quite in keeping with the general air of the man. His hands, large and coarse, were plentifully bedecked with rings; and he wore a heavy gold watch-chain, with a bundle of seals of portentous size, and a great variety of colors, attached to it,—which, in the ardor of conversation, he was in the habit of flourishing and jingling with evident satisfaction. His conversation was in free and easy defiance of Murray's Grammar, and was garnished at convenient intervals with various profane expressions. (41–42)

Stowe often identifies characters thus as examples of types, or she makes generalizations about particular species of human beings. Mrs. Shelby, for example, is described as being "a woman of high class, both intellectually and morally. To that natural magnanimity and generosity of mind which one often marks as characteristic of the women of Kentucky, she added high moral and religious sensibility and principle, carried out with great energy and ability into practical results" (52). Thus, Mrs. Shelby is a variant on the type "the women of Kentucky," who are known for their "natural magnanimity and generosity of mind." On the next page, Stowe similarly describes "quadroon and mulatto women" as having a "peculiar air of refinement" and a "softness of voice and manner." In the quadroon "these natural graces . . . are often united with beauty of the most dazzling kind" (54).[1] Stowe uses this generalization to introduce Eliza, who, though based supposedly on a real person, is true to type.

These kinds of generalizations grate for the modern reader, who is more sensitive than Stowe to the destructive purposes to which such racial stereotypes have been put. Indeed, fixing a person as a representative of a type is a kind of reification or objectification, which Stowe otherwise deplores. Nevertheless, it is clear that Stowe uses these generic sweeps only as broad strokes on her canvas and does not intend that they be taken too seriously. Often in fact they are for comic effect. And despite her regularly identifying figures as types, the characters themselves are usually individualized, so that few are actually stereotypes.

Uncle Tom himself is not introduced until chapter 4, but his character is indicated in the opening pages—again from the viewpoint of the slave traders, presented ironically, who are appraising his virtues as commodities while they haggle over his price. "Tom is an uncommon fellow; he is certainly worth that sum anywhere,—steady, honest, capable, manages my whole farm like a clock," Shelby brags (420). To reinforce his point and to up the price, Shelby tells an anecdote that illustrates Tom's extraordinary loyalty and honesty. The preceding fall Shelby sent Tom to Cincinnati alone to carry out a business transaction where Tom was entrusted with five hundred dollars, which he returned with. Such an expedition obviously gave Tom a royal opportunity to escape, but as a Christian he felt he could not go back on his word to return to his master (43). This is one of many episodes that black critics have criticized (see chapter 3), but apparently it is based on real incidents Stowe had read or heard about, and in any event, the Christian slave was a familiar figure in slave narratives. *The Life of Josiah Henson* (1849) contains a similar episode, but as Charles Foster points out, Henson is an obsequious opportunistic collaborator, whereas

Tom is not. Stowe also mentioned two other sources for Tom's Christian behavior: one, the husband of her Cincinnati cook, Eliza Buck, who refused to run away from his master because he trusted the latter to free him. The second Stowe mentions in *The Key to "Uncle Tom's Cabin"* having learned about "in an obscure town in Maine" (Brunswick?) from a person who had visited in New Orleans and heard about a slave known for his loyalty and piety.[2]

The opening scene, which takes place on a "chilly" afternoon in February, also reveals other aspects of the white-black relationship under slavery. As noted, Eliza is introduced through the eyes of the slave trader, who immediately sees her as a sexual commodity. "[T]here's an article, now! You might make your fortune on that ar gal in Orleans, any day. I've seen over a thousand in my day, paid down for gals not a bit handsomer" (45). (It was this kind of detail, incidentally, that scandalized especially southern critics of the novel, who thought it was improprietous for Stowe to know or to reveal that she knew about such goings on.)

Mr. Shelby's treatment of Harry, Eliza's five-year-old son, exemplifies white condescension toward blacks. "Hullo, Jim Crow!" Shelby calls to him, "whistling and snapping a bunch of raisins towards him." After the boy dutifully scampers after the raisins, "the master patted the curly head, and chucked him under the chin," as one would a dog (44). The term *Jim Crow* derived from a Negro character in nineteenth-century minstrel acts; it is used here to get the boy to do some tricks of mimicry. The slavetrader Haley is so impressed that he agrees to throw Harry into the bargain and call off Shelby's debt.

As the chapter concludes, the boy's mother, Eliza, having figured out that something is afoot, asks Mrs. Shelby if the master would sell her child. Mrs. Shelby, then unaware of the deal, assures her that they would never consider it.

In the next three chapters we enter the black world—the realm of Uncle Tom's cabin, where we encounter *Life among the Lowly,* the novel's subtitle. Although the scenes are relatively happy and the slaves are seen to have a relatively independent culture of their own, their reality is undercut by the dramatic irony established in the opening scene. Without their knowledge decisions have been made in the antithetical white world that will control their fates henceforth. Thus the irony that pervades these chapters is created, once again, by the rhetorical principle of antithesis, the clash between two worlds and two sets of characters with variant purposes: whites wanting to use blacks as commodities for their own economic purposes; blacks wanting to live their lives as free subjects.

Before we reach the cabin of Tom and Chloe, however, we are introduced to George and Eliza Harris, a slave husband and wife who are also antithetical characters parallel to the polarized white couple on the plantation, Mr. and Mrs. Shelby. Their private discussion is a dialectical debate similar to that held in chapter 5 by the Shelbys. In each case the woman proposes a gentler, more humane course, and the man, a more destructive, violent one.

Eliza, unfortunately, is not a well-developed character. She is something of a sentimentalist stereotype: the devoted mother and kindly Christian. Like others of this type she exudes goodness but is often a victim. Eliza is perhaps somewhat more fearful and anxious than the usual type, but with good reason. Through most of the novel she is underground, in flight.

George, on the other hand, is more individualized and therefore more interesting. Assertive, bright, and rebellious, he expresses a cynical atheism that contrasts directly to his wife's timid Christianity. Unlike Eliza, who, under Mrs. Shelby's aegis, has led a rather sheltered life, George has personally experienced much injustice and brutality. Although he invented a hemp-cleaning machine, comparable, according to Stowe, to the cotton gin, he received no reward or recognition from his master, who instead became jealous of George's success and forced him to perform more menial heavy farm labor. Despite the fact that "a whole volcano of bitter feelings burned in [George's] bosom" (56), the master is intransigent, saying, ironically, "it's a free country . . . the man's *mine,* and I do what I please with him" (57). Meanwhile, Eliza lost two children in infancy, which has made her particularly attached to the only child who survives, Harry.

In a lengthy discussion in Eliza's apartment, George reveals himself to be suicidally depressed with his plight. Beaten regularly and seething with the injustice of having an ignorant man keep him from the creative intellectual projects he is capable of, he grows increasingly rebellious. Eliza counsels Christian submission, but as noted in chapter 4, George rejects a god who can allow such evil to exist. The final straw is when his master refuses to let George visit Eliza (they live on neighboring plantations and legally slaves could not marry), whereupon George decides to flee to Canada and earn enough money to buy Eliza and Harry's freedom.

After this tearful and fearful scene, Stowe switches to the benign contentment of Tom and Chloe's cabin. This small log structure, surrounded by flowers and "a neat garden-patch" (66) is somewhat idyllic, indeed edenic; like the Quaker home described in chapter 13, it provides a glimpse of Stowe's utopian vision of an alternative society. Despite being called "Uncle Tom's cabin," the province is ruled over by Aunt Chloe, one of Stowe's great matriarchal characters, similar in many respects to the monumental Grandmother Badger, a white New Englander, in *Oldtown Folks* (1869). Like her, Aunt Chloe exudes confidence and competence, is authoritarian but indulgent, proud but jovial. She is a power by the force of her personality. She jokes and puts down the white "master" George, the thirteen-year-old Shelby son, who is visiting in the cabin, and she even has been known to order Mrs. Shelby around. Once when the latter was meddling in her kitchen, Chloe was "sarcy" enough to ask her to leave (72).

There is a sense of permanence about Chloe and her world, as if the domestic rituals over which she presides have gone on for ages and will (and should) continue uninterrupted into the indefinite future. Stowe establishes this sense by taking the reader into the cabin as Chloe is preparing supper in "her own snug territories," having finished managing the evening meal in "the house" of the Shelbys. "Let us enter the dwelling," Stowe recommends. "[D]oubt not that it is her you see by the fire, presiding with anxious interest over certain frizzling items in a stew-pan, and anon with grave consideration lifting the cover of a bake-kettle" (66). The solid, secure domesticity of this scene makes the impending violation of it, wrought by the sale of Chloe's husband, Uncle Tom, seem all the more horrible. Stowe probably calculated that most of her readers would be whites who knew little about blacks and were perhaps even fearful of them; so to counter this she sought to familiarize their world to the white reader. Seeing Chloe and Tom in a peaceful, comfortable kitchen setting would, of course, do just that.[3]

But even in this relatively harmonious environment, the shadow of slavery looms. Chloe has to serve "Master George," the Shelbys' son, the choice pieces of the meal before she serves her own children or husband. Young George is there teaching Tom to write—a painful reminder of the slaves' lack of education. In watching George form his letters Aunt Chloe observes, "How easy white folks al'us does things!" (69)—an ironic comment in view of the fact that she is at the time skillfully "greasing a griddle" (69). Since she is known as the best cook in the area, the comment ironically juxtaposes two competencies—mental and manual, another example of Stowe's antithetical style.

Uncle Tom, "the hero of our story" (68), is introduced in this domestic context. His wife cooking at the stove, children clambering in the corner, Tom is laboriously engaged in shaping letters, as we first encounter him. (Significantly Tom is referred to as "Uncle Tom" only at the Shelby plantation; elsewhere in the novel he is simply Tom or, briefly at the Legree plantation, "Father Tom.") "He was a large, broad-chested, powerfully-made man, of a full glossy black, and a face whose truly African features were characterized by an expression of grave and steady good sense, united with much kindliness and benevolence. There was something about his whole air self-respecting and dignified, yet united with a confiding and humble simplicity" (68). It is important to stress here—in light of the egregious misinterpretation of his character that has been perpetrated in popular culture—that Tom is a physically strong, relatively young, large man, who has a "self-respecting and dignified," if humble air. That he is wholly African—rather than a mulatto like Eliza and George—is significant for a number of reasons. One is that, as noted, Stowe believed in inherent racial traits and therefore that a full-blooded African would be more likely to exhibit these characteristics than one whose ancestry included whites, particularly what Stowe disparagingly called "Anglo-Saxons."

Africans, Stowe felt, were gentle and domestic (162), timid and patient (165), and not inclined to be risk-taking adventurers or entrepreneurs (164) (and therefore not inclined toward capitalism). They were also kindly (231). They were more ethically and aesthetically sensitive than whites (418, 430) and therefore more naturally religious (342). They were, in short, considerably more attractive than Anglo-Saxons, whom Stowe saw generally as a more masculine, a "more coldly and strictly logical race,"[4] one given to dominance and violence (392). (Stowe also saw other "races" in stereotypical ways: "The French and the Spanish nations are, by constitution, more impulsive, passionate, and poetic, than logical.")[5]

Stowe clearly considered Africans the last, best hope of humanity—they were the chosen people with whom God had made a special covenant. Here Stowe was adapting the Calvinist idea that God's covenant was with the New England Puritans. The utopian "city on a hill" dreamt of in the Puritan imagination was in Stowe's vision transposed to Africa. Later in the novel she prophesies:

> life will awake there with a gorgeousness and splendor of which our cold western tribes faintly have conceived. In that far-off mystic land of gold, gems, and species, and waving palms, and wondrous flowers, and miraculous fertility, will awake new forms of art, new styles of splendor; and the negro race, no longer despised and trodden down, will, perhaps, show forth some of the latest and most magnificent revelations of human life. Certainly they will, in their gentleness, their lowly docility of heart, their aptitude to repose on a superior mind and rest on a higher power [here Stowe means God, not whites], their childlike simplicity of affection, and facility of forgiveness. In all these they will exhibit the highest form of the peculiarly *Christian life*, and perhaps, as God chasteneth whom he loveth, he hath chosen poor Africa in the furnace of affliction, to make her the highest and noblest in that kingdom which he will set up, when every other kingdom has been tried, and failed; for the first shall be last, and the last first. (275)

It is within the context of these theories of African superiority that we must see the character Uncle Tom. He exhibits the characteristics of his race, undiluted by the meaner traits of the Anglo-Saxons. One of the reasons for George's contrasting temperament—his prideful rebelliousness and inclination toward atheism and violence—is his Anglo-Saxon blood (182). Tom, on the other hand, remains a model Christian in part, at least, because of his African heritage. It is then perhaps ironic that George lives to become a founding father of the African utopia Stowe describes above, rather than Tom, who is more temperamentally suited to the peaceful world Stowe envisages. But by the end of the novel George has repudiated his Anglo-Saxon ancestry and embraced Stowe's vision for a Christian Africa (608–12). Had Stowe made Tom a George Washington instead of a Christ, we would have a very different novel—a utopian novel that elides the problem of evil. Since Stowe's principal purpose was, we have stressed, to address the problem of evil, this was not the novel she wished to write. Hence Tom's resolute facing of evil, rather than escaping it, is critical to the novel's integrity, giving it a moral significance beyond period utopian fiction.

Tom's leadership capabilities are, however, seen in the opening episodes, which include a black religious revival meeting, a weekly occurrence held in the cabin. "The room . . . filled with a motley assemblage, from the old gray-headed patriarch of eighty, to the young girl and lad of fifteen. A little harmless gossip ensued on various themes. . . . After a while the singing commenced" (77). Some historians, notably Eugene Genovese, have seen black slave Christianity as "a religion of resistance—not often of revolutionary defiance, but of a spiritual resistance." An important element in black Christian worship was the prayer meeting held in peoples' homes (as seen here in *Uncle Tom's Cabin*).[6]

Gospel singing was clearly an important part of the service. The Methodist hymns Stowe cites express the "anticipatory illumination" Ernst Bloch recognized as characteristic of the utopian vision. A "special favorite" repeated the words *"Don't you see the golden city and the everlasting day?"* As Stowe notes, the hymns made "incessant mention of 'Jordan's banks,' and 'Canaan's fields,' and the 'New Jerusalem' " (78). "[A]s they sung, some laughed, and some cried, and some clapped hands, or shook hands rejoicingly with each other, as if they had fairly gained the other side of the river" (78). These projections of a fulfilled afterlife comment dialectically on the downtrodden lives the slaves were enduring, and, undoubtedly, as Genovese suggests, such collective imaginative projections must have been psychologically empowering for the slaves.

After the singing, members of the congregation engaged in recitals of personal witness or "exhortations." These were "often interrupted by such exclamations as 'The *sakes* now!' 'Only hear that!' 'Just think ot 't!' 'Is all that comin' sure enough?' " (78).

Uncle Tom was "a sort of minister among them" being "a sort of patriarch in religious matters, in the neighborhood" (79). This was because of his "strongly predominant" ethical sense but also because he had "a greater breadth and cultivation of mind" than the others; "he was [therefore] looked up to with great respect" (79). His unofficial sermons are marked by a "hearty, sincere style," and "nothing could exceed the touching simplicity, the child-like earnestness, of his prayer, enriched with the language of Scripture, which seemed so entirely to have wrought itself into his being, as to have become a part of himself, and to drop from his lips unconsciously" (79). In other words, Tom's religion is unmediated; he speaks in a pure, uncontaminated way, in direct connection with the heart's truth, with God. Tom is thus, from the point of view of Edwardsean Calvinism, one of God's elect.

Near the end of chapter 4, which has covered this "Evening in Uncle Tom's Cabin" (the chapter title), Stowe switches abruptly back to the big house, where at the moment of the prayer meeting, the bill of Tom's sale is being signed by Mr. Shelby—another dramatic example of Stowe's method of antithetical juxtaposition for ironic purpose.

Before returning there, however, I would like to digress—in the manner of Stowe herself—to consider briefly Stowe's use of dialect. One of the hallmarks of realism in the nineteenth century, especially the "local color" realism that Stowe pioneered in her early stories, was the use of authentic dialect, appropriate to characters' region and class. *Uncle Tom's Cabin* was the first novel to present a sustained representation of relatively authentic Negro dialect. The plantation novelists of the 1830s had made some effort at capturing black dialect, but the slave narratives, because they were in the first person, used little dialect, nor did the abolition novels. According to E. Bruce Kirkham, Stowe reworked the Negro dialect considerably between the journal publication of the novel and its book publication in an attempt at greater accuracy. An authority on dialect claims she was "makeshift" with her use of dialect, however, and was careless and inconsistent in its use, though she "sometimes obtained" "excellent effects." In her later work, *The Minister's Wooing,* for example, the black dialect is more accurate. Generally, Stowe's characters speak as one might expect: educated blacks speak standard English, as do the middle- and upper-class whites (there is no attempt to capture a southern accent in white southern characters). Lower-class and rural whites speak in dialect and slang, and less-educated blacks speak in field or house-servant dialect, depending on their status. Tom, for example, speaks in a mixture of field- and house-servant dialect, as well as in standard English often using biblical diction.[7] The Quakers use the familiar "Thee" and "Thou" form.

Meanwhile, back at the "big house," Mr. and Mrs. Shelby are engaging in a heated debate over the prospective sale. It is evening and Mrs. Shelby is brushing out her hair in their "apartment." (It is worth noting, in view of comments made by recent critics Brown and Spillers that white women's sexuality is largely repressed in the novel, that Mrs. Shelby's first two appearances are vaguely sensual and narcissistic [52, 81]; but it is true that white women are rarely seen in these terms in the work—whatever that may imply.) As noted earlier, the Shelbys have antithetical opinions about the sale. She reacts to the news with shocked disbelief, while he maintains it is a regrettable matter of business. She then expresses abolitionist sentiment, saying slavery is a "deadly evil" (84) and that she was a fool to think she could mitigate its effects by kindly behavior. She vows that she will be "in no sense accomplice or help in this cruel business" (86), and that instead she will aid Tom and Eliza—thus establishing what Monrose

Gwin has labeled the novel's "feminist subtext," where white women bond with black women, usually in response to a "male-initiated crisis." Mrs. Shelby, though she had "racist presumptions" in that she treats blacks condescendingly, exhibits genuine love, empathy, and compassion for black women—in particular Eliza and Aunt Chloe. "Mrs. Shelby's loyalty to Eliza actually supercedes her loyalty to her husband."[8]

Eliza, once again, overhears the conversation between the Shelbys and resolves to flee immediately with Harry. As she slips out into the night, she stops by Uncle Tom's cabin to tell him the dreadful news. Chloe urges Tom to escape with Eliza, but Tom refuses, seeing himself in sacrificial terms. "If I must be sold, or all the people on the place, and everything go to the rack, why let me be sold. I s'pose I can b'ar it as well as any on 'em. . . . It's better for me alone to go, than to break up the place and sell all." Whereupon he bursts into "sobs, heavy, hoarse and loud" (90). Thus, while Tom also mentions as a reason for not escaping that he has never "broke trust" (90), his principal position is that his sale will save the rest of the slaves, allowing them to remain in the benign security of the Shelby estate. It is a Christ-like act that prefigures his status at the novel's end.

7

Middle Ground

The main transitions in *Uncle Tom's Cabin* occur on the great inland American waterways—the Ohio River, the Mississippi River, the Red River, and Lake Erie—giving the novel what Ellen Moers called "its great river structure."[1] Eliza's flight across the Ohio is one of the most famous scenes in the novel. Her hair-raising scramble across blocks of ice in the river—apparently based on a real incident[2]—has become a set piece in American popular culture, well known to people who have never read the novel.

After leaving the Shelby plantation, Eliza makes it to the Kentucky side of the river without being discovered, all the while clutching to her the child Harry. Because she is very light-skinned, Eliza is able to "pass" as white and thus secure a room in an inn near the river. (George, her husband, is also a light-skinned mulatto and also thus able to pass, as we shall see shortly. Stowe has been criticized for allowing the mulattos to escape, while sacrificing the darker Tom. But it was a historical fact that light-skinned blacks had a better chance to escape undetected.) Eliza had hoped to get a ferry across the river, but her pursuer, the slave trader Haley, catches up with her before the boat is scheduled to leave, so she desperately races out a side door of the inn and descends the riverbank, just as Haley catches sight of her. Driven by "madness and despair" she leaps onto a "huge green fragment of ice," which "pitched and creaked as her weight came on it," and then hopscotches across the river, the child in her arms, finally reaching the Ohio shore, as her pursuers back in Kentucky watch "perfectly amazed" (118–19). She is helped up the Ohio bank to a safe haven by a man who, Stowe remarks sarcastically, "had not been instructed in his constitutional relations"—an allusion to the Fugitive Slave Law, according to which he should have returned her to Kentucky (119). The dramatic tension of these scenes shows why Stowe is considered among the great storytellers of all time. Indeed, it is the sustained narrative suspense of the novel that probably accounts in large part for its popular success.

Meanwhile, Stowe describes, in essentially comic scenes, the turmoil and confusion that resulted at the Shelby plantation when Eliza's escape is discovered. Mrs. Shelby exclaims, "the Lord be thanked," when she hears the news, which Andy, one of the servants, reports (92). The black reaction to Eliza's escape is one of exuberance; a number of the slaves engage in taunting Haley. Black Sam, however, realizes that his star will rise as Tom's falls because he is likely to be Tom's replacement and thus receive Tom's privileges. To show his mettle, Sam vows to please the master by catching Eliza; Andy, however, warns him "you'd better think twice; for Missis don't want her cotched, and she'll be in yer wool" (96). Sam and Andy, therefore, with Mrs. Shelby's encouragement sabotage the pursuit of Eliza. Sam puts a nut under Haley's horse's saddle, so the horse throws Haley and is further spooked—along with the other horses—when Sam waves his palm-leaf hat at them. The horses run off, pandemonium ensues, and the chase after Eliza is considerably delayed. When the party finally does get organized, further postponed by Chloe's dilatory preparation of dinner and Mrs. Shelby's dallying tactics during the meal, it is led astray by Sam and Andy, which enables Eliza to escape.

Although somewhat stereotypical (they probably established the Amos and Andy types), Sam and Andy are amusing characters whose behavior is at times farcical. On his return to the plantation with the good news of Eliza's escape, Sam gives a burlesque political oration to the other slaves, addressing them as "fellow-countrymen" (138), embellishing his role in the affair. When Andy reminds him that his decision to aid Eliza had been based on expediency, Sam rebukes him saying it was a matter of conscience. "When I found Missis was sot the contrar [to catching Eliza], dat ar was conscience *more yet*,—cause fellers allers gets more by stickin' to Missis' side" (139). In the end, Sam acknowledges that for him principle lies in being "persistent in wantin' to get up which ary side my larder is" (139). Stowe tartly comments that Sam could have been an eminent politician (136).

Scenes such as this and the revival meeting treated in the preceding chapter give the reader a vivid sense of the reality of slave life. One critic has suggested that *Uncle Tom's Cabin* conveys "a sense of the vitality" of slave life greater than the slave narratives and other fiction of the period.[3] Probably this is because of Stowe's great pictorial talent and panoramic scope; the slave narratives tended to focus on one person's unhappy experiences from that individual's point of view. Stowe realized that no one would read a novel that was relentlessly grim (indeed *Uncle Tom's Cabin* outsold all of the slave narratives and abolition novels put together); and so she deliberately interposed pleasant and comic scenes. She remarked, "The writer acknowledges that the book is a very inadequate representation of slavery [because] slavery, in some of its workings, is too dreadful for the purposes of art. A work which should represent it strictly as it is would be a work which could not be read; and all works which ever mean to give pleasure must draw a veil somewhere, or they cannot succeed." In fiction, therefore, one can "find refuge from the hard and the terrible, by inventing scenes and characters of a more pleasing nature," but she insisted, in reality "there is no bright-side to slavery."[4]

Stowe raises some interesting aesthetic issues here, particularly how art relates to great moral and political evils. Anticipating Theodor Adorno's comment that there could be no poetry after Auschwitz, Stowe believed that although literature could not adequately represent an atrocious evil such as slavery, it could be used to combat it. Thus, in her view the aesthetic dimension of literature was always subservient to the moral. In a letter to George Eliot, Stowe wrote that she had "enjoyed reading" *Middlemarch*. "As *art* it is perfect, but perfect art as an end—not instrument—has little to interest me." To Anna Dickinson, she wrote, "Don't mind what anybody says about [your novel] as a work of art. Works of art be hanged! You had a better thought than that."[5] Thus, the aesthetically pleasing alteration of light and dark scenes in *Uncle Tom's Cabin* has the ultimate purpose of keeping the reader reading and thus persuading her or him of slavery's injustice. The comical scene with Sam is followed in the narrative by the more serious events at Senator and Mrs. Bird's home in Cincinnati, where Eliza is harbored briefly on her transit north and where Stowe's endorsement of civil disobedience and philosophical advocacy of a personalist ethic is presented (see discussion in chapter 5).

Stowe's skill as a realist is perhaps most evident in the tavern scenes of chapters 8 and 11. (Her unladylike knowledge of these public, masculine spaces also scandalized a few early critics.) In a masterful scene that exudes sardonic humor, Stowe describes the slave catchers, Tom Loker and Marks, his antithetical sidekick. These events occur in chapter 8, the only chapter to be untitled in the original first edition of the novel.[6]

Loker and Marks happen to arrive at the Kentucky tavern where Haley is fuming over the loss of his property, Harry. Loker, "standing by the bar . . . was a brawny, muscular man, full six feet in height, and broad in proportion. He was dressed in a coat of buffalo-skin, made with the hair outward, which gave him a shaggy and fierce appearance . . . expressive of brutal and unhesitating violence." His counterpart, by contrast, "was short and slender, lithe and catlike in his motions, and had a peering, mousing expression about his keen black eyes . . . ; his sleek, thin, black hair was stuck eagerly forward." While Loker "poured out a big tumbler half full of raw spirits . . . the little man stood tip-toe, and . . . ordered at last a mint julep [a somewhat effeminate drink], in a thin and quavering voice, and with an air of great circumspection" (122).

Descriptions such as these, which the novel is replete in, are an example of what I earlier labeled Stowe's "creatural realism." They serve no particular purpose in advancing the plot or even in hammering home Stowe's moral purpose (other than entertaining readers and therefore keeping them hooked). Rather they express a certain comic exuberance on Stowe's part for the diversity of humanity, a certain delight in its eccentricity. This "attentive love" for the diversity of creation is an aspect of her Christianity and, as noted, connects to a moral sensitivity that values individual particularities and refuses to erase them as irrelevant. Of this kind of sensitivity contemporary British novelist and philosopher Iris Murdoch once wrote, "the more the separateness and differentness of other people is realized . . . the harder it becomes to treat a person as a thing." It is this kind of realism, she continued, that "makes great art great."[7] Certainly an important aspect of *Uncle Tom's Cabin*'s claims to greatness and one of its chief delights (also seen in her other novels) is Stowe's enthusiastic immersion in eccentric details of personality, such as the bizarre character, Marks, just described.

Despite his simpering style, however, Marks is a slave trader, and he, Loker, and Haley spend the evening complaining about the difficulties of their profession, exchanging brutal stories about recalcitrant "articles," mainly mothers who refuse to give up their children gracefully. Haley reveals that eventually he plans to repent and tend to his soul, but Loker scoffs, "take a bright look-out to find a soul in you. . . . If the devil sifts you through a hair sieve, he won't find one" (126). Through the course of the scene we learn Loker and Marks's modus operandi; the latter poses before northern justices as a southern gentleman attempting to retrieve his property, while Loker's job is to round up the property. Marks explains, "One day I'm Mr. Twickem, from New Orleans; 'nother day, I'm just come from my plantation on Pearl river, where I works seven hundred niggers; then, again, I come out a distant relation of Henry Clay, or some old cock in Kentuck. Talents is different, you know" (128). In enumerating their various contracts Marks explains, some are "easy cases, 'cause all you've got to do is shoot 'em, or swear they is shot" (131). Stowe sarcastically concludes this scene by remarking, "If any of our refined and Christian readers object to the society into which this scene introduced them, . . .

the catching business, we beg to remind them, is rising to the dignity of a lawful and patriotic profession," an allusion to the Fugitive Slave Law. She continues, if slave trading is extended into the territories west of the Mississippi, making it "one great market for bodies and souls," "the trader and catcher may yet be among our aristocracy" (132)— this because, Stowe suggests, capitalism determines the composition of American classes.

Another tavern scene occurs in chapter 11. Here the protagonist is George Harris, daringly disguised as a wealthy Spanish-looking aristocrat named Henry Butler. He is accompanied by a "servant," Jim, another fugitive slave, who is attempting to rescue his mother from slavery via the underground railway. Once again the setting is a barroom: "rifles stacked away in the corner, shot-pouches, game-bags, hunting-dogs, and little negroes, all rolled together in the corners,— were the characteristic features in the picture" (175).

A new arrival, Mr. Wilson, who had owned the factory where George had invented the hemp machine, reads a wanted poster describing George and advertising his escape; it concludes, *"I will give four hundred dollars for him alive, and the same sum for satisfactory proof that he has been killed"* (178). One of the barroom guests spits tobacco on it, and a discussion about slavery ensues.

George himself arrives on the scene (in disguise) and coolly saunters over to the poster, commenting to his servant, "with a careless yawn," "seems to me we met a boy something like this, up at Bernan's didn't we?" (181). Meanwhile, Mr. Wilson gradually recognizes him, but George addresses him directly, and, once in the privacy of George's room, he agrees to keep George's secret—thus himself committing civil disobedience. George's philosophy is further developed in this chapter. Not only does he reject the idea of submission to Providence that Wilson counsels, saying that in his case such would be suicidal, he also rejects the authority of the U.S. government, insisting that he has no country because he has none of the rights of citizenship. George thus applies the natural rights doctrine to himself, noting that as a slave he has no say in the formulation of laws. If "governments derive their just power from the consent of the governed," then the current government has no legitimacy for blacks (185). This argument, of course, is derived from the Declaration of Independence, where it was used to authorize revolution. Similarly, George exclaims, "I'll fight for my liberty to the last breath I breathe. . . . [I]f it was right for [the founding fathers], it is right for me!" (187). Armed with two pistols and a bowie knife, George is prepared to use violence if necessary. Thus, George provides a philosophical counterpoint to Uncle Tom, another example of Stowe's paired antithetical characters. Where the latter preaches nonviolent Christian submission, George advocates a violent assertion of one's rights and disbelieves in a just God.

Meanwhile, back at the Shelby plantation, Uncle Tom is taking his leave (this section, covered in chapters 10 and 12, will be treated in the next chapter), and in Ohio (unknown to George) Eliza is being escorted through the agency of Senator and Mrs. Bird and John Van Trompe to a Quaker settlement—a station on the underground railroad. (Stowe herself, by the way, was a part of such a network in Cincinnati, helping many fugitive slaves to escape north. She remarked to one correspondent, "time would fail to tell you all that I learned incidentally of the slave system in the history of various slaves who came into my family, and of the underground railroad which, I may say, ran through our house."[8])

Like Mrs. Shelby, Mrs. Bird, another white woman, is instrumental in facilitating Eliza's passage to safety. Mrs. Bird, who is still mourning over the death of a child, is deeply empathetic with Eliza's fear of losing Harry. On hearing Eliza's frightening story she (and everyone else within range) is moved to tears, except that, Stowe sarcastically notes, the "senator was a statesman, and of course could not be expected to cry, like other mortals" (150). Once again, Stowe here is criticizing abstractions like duty, country, and statesmanship that tend to force the individual to repress personal emotional responses that might otherwise be an ethical guide. Then, as now, of course, men were expected to do more of this repression in the name of duty and service to the country than women, which Stowe, as a cultural feminist, saw as a critical ethical problem. Were men to learn from women not to suppress their feelings, aroused by individual instances of suffering and evil, in the name of various legitimizing abstractions, we would be well on the way, she felt, toward a more humane society—and certainly one that did not countenance slavery. As noted in chapter 5, this thesis, so central to *Uncle Tom's Cabin,* is endorsed by many feminists today (see chapter 5, n. 2).

Thus, Mrs. Bird loans her dead son's clothes to Harry, and Mr. Bird, impelled by "the real presence of distress," drives Eliza (aided by his servant Cudjoe) to the home of John Van Trompe—another suspenseful transit scene that is punctuated by various carriage mishaps.

The next time we encounter Eliza and Harry (chapter 13), they are securely ensconced in the Quaker home of the Hallidays—a central image of the peaceable kingdom in the work (along with the Bird home and the cabin of Tom and Chloe). Eliza is pictured sewing on a "motherly" old chair, "whose wide arms breathed hospitable invitation." She is in a "a large, roomy, neatly-painted kitchen, its yellow floor glossy and smooth, and without a particle of dust; a neat, well-blacked cooking-stove, rows of shining tin, suggestive of unmentionable good things to the appetite" (214).

By her side "sorting some dried peaches" is the Quaker woman Rachel Halliday, dressed in the typical Quaker outfit ("the snowy lisse crape cap, . . . the plain white muslin handkerchief, . . . the drab shawl and dress") (215). She is in her late fifties. Like Tom and Eva, the other Christian exemplars in the novel, Rachel's goodness is unmediated. "[Y]ou only needed to look straight into" her "clear, honest, loving brown eyes" to "feel that you saw to the bottom of a heart as good and true as ever throbbed" (215). In her "twenty years or more" as a mother, "nothing but loving words, and gentle moralities, and motherly loving kindness" had come from her: "headaches and heart-aches innumerable had been cured . . . difficulties spiritual and temporal solved . . . all by one good, loving woman" (216).

As in the scenes with little Eva, the modern reader may find tedious or at least improbable the relentless cheer and goodwill of the characters in the Quaker community. There is indeed a certain artificiality about their behavior. For example, when Rachel, her husband, Simeon, and a neighbor Ruth discover that George Harris is in the community, they

UNCLE TOM'S CABIN

debate whether to tell Eliza or not (why they don't tell her right off is, of course, a question; it may reflect a certain racist condescension). Ruth says that if it were her husband, she would want to know right away, so they should tell Eliza immediately that George has arrived. Simeon comments, "Thee uses thyself only to learn how to love thy neighbor, Ruth." Ruth replies, "To be sure. . . . If I didn't love John [her husband] and the baby, I should not know how to feel for her" (220). This kind of acute self-consciousness seems improbable; it is clear that Stowe wanted to make the point that personal connections and empathetic analogy form an important basis for ethical behavior—and once again it is a mother's ties that provide the ground for empathy, but Stowe's use of her characters here is heavy-handed. Their self-reflectiveness makes their behavior seem studied and self-congratulatory rather than natural. In short, they are puppets being used by Stowe to make a moral point. (They do finally tell Eliza, and she is reunited with George in the Halliday home. They remain together with their son through the ensuing flight to Canada.)

On the other hand, the Quaker community provides an important glimpse of Stowe's notion of utopia. It is a matriarchal, domestic province, remarkable for its egalitarian humanism, for the "I-Thou" character of relationships, its orderly cleanliness, and its prodigal bounty, fairly apportioned. Economically, it is a world of use-value production, to use Marxist terms, where goods are produced and consumed by the immediate community, as opposed to modern industrial production (seen at the Legree plantation) where commodities are manufactured for their abstract exchange value.[9] Work is done collectively; men and older children share in some of the household chores. In preparing the breakfast, for example: "John ran to the spring for fresh water, and Simeon the second sifted meal for corn-cakes, and Mary ground coffee" (222). Rachel mediates among the workers, ensuring that the process runs "harmoniously" (223). George and Eliza are treated as equals at the breakfast table—a new experience for them—and the former's "misanthropic, pining atheistic doubts, and fierce despair, melted away before the light of the living gospel" (224).

Rachel's kitchen provides an important counterpoint to the corrupt worlds further south, which we encounter later in the novel—Dinah's disorderly kitchen at the St. Clare plantation and the dissolute profanity of the Legree estate, where no one is treated fairly and slaves are mere mechanisms, on the edge of starvation and subject to arbitrary tyranny.

But even this kitchen scene is marred by such rhetorical excesses as "the chicken and ham had a cheerful and joyous fizzle in the pan, as if they rather enjoyed being cooked than otherwise"—obvious nonsense that makes the modern reader wince. In an evident attempt to justify Stowe's saccharine hyperbole here, Jane Tompkins argues that one must understand that these scenes are charged with religious significance. Rachel, she claims, is an apotheosis; she is "God in human form. Seated in her kitchen at the head of her table, passing out coffee and cake for breakfast, Rachel Halliday, the millenarian counterpart of little Eva, enacts the redeemed form of the Last Supper. This is Holy Communion as it will be under the new dispensation." Tompkins theorizes that *Uncle Tom's Cabin* is the "summa theologica of nineteenth-century America's religion of domesticity . . . the story of salvation through motherly love."[10]

Tompkins is surely right to point out the religious and thematic significance of this scene, but the words *Last Supper, Holy Communion,* and *summa theologica* suggest a weighty patriarchal tradition, rather the opposite of what Stowe is trying to convey. Instead, Stowe's point seems to be that apparently minor and trivial domestic rituals, such as breakfast, have a sacred character and that indeed this kind of everyday sharing of being among equals is the most important counterweight to evil available. Stowe's ultimate vision here is of a kind of existential religion.

8

Transitions South

In Stowe's counterpoint construction the comic upbeat scenes at the Birds (chapter 9), in the taverns (8 and 11), and at the Halliday's (13) alternate with grimmer and darker scenes further south, where Tom makes his agonizing departure from the Shelby plantation (chapter 10) and begins his journey to New Orleans with slave trader Haley. On the way we are exposed to a slave auction and to the transport of slaves as cargo on a Mississippi riverboat (12).

Chapter 10, ironically entitled "In Which the Property Is Carried Off," returns us to Uncle Tom's cabin for his "last supper" (actually it's breakfast) at home with his wife and children. As Chloe, sobbing, irons his clothes for the trip, and as Tom reads his Bible and plays with his infant daughter, the two engage in a philosophical debate over what the proper attitude toward this unhappy event should be. Tom, of course, adopts an attitude of Christian resignation and martyrdom. He is glad that it is he who is being sold down the river and not the others. But Aunt Chloe's position is closer to George Harris's; she is bristling at the injustice of Mr. Shelby's behavior. "Mas'r never ought ter left it so that ye *could* be took for his debts. Ye've arnt him all he gets for ye, twice over. He owed ye yer freedom, and ought ter gin 't to yer years ago. Mebbe he can't help himself now, but I feel it's wrong. . . . Them as sells heart's love and heart's blood, to get out thar scrapes, de Lord'll be up to 'em!" (163). Thus, Chloe remarks that the fundamental injustice of slavery—that "masters" reap profits from the slaves' labor—is here compounded by Shelby's failure to have the basic decency to reward Tom for his years of extraordinary service. Such treachery, Chloe feels, will provoke God's wrath.

Tom, however, in a gesture that some might find too sympathetic to his oppressor, defends Shelby by saying he was brought up to be insensitive and therefore his behavior is understandable. "[H]e couldn't be spected to think so much of poor Tom. Mas'rs is used to havin' all these yer things done for 'em, and nat'lly they don't think so much on 't. They can't be spected to, no way" (164). But Chloe insists that whatever the explanation and whatever Shelby's motivations, "thar's wrong about it *somewhar*. . . . I'm *clar* o' that" (164).

Just before Tom's departure Mrs. Shelby comes down to the cabin to express her sympathy. Understandably, Chloe is somewhat annoyed at the intrusion, saying, "She can't do no good; what's she coming for?" She expresses her irritation by setting a chair for Mrs. Shelby in "a manner decidedly gruff and crusty" (167). (I think Stowe has to be credited here with taking the point of view of the black woman, rather than sweeping her away in a rush of enthusiasm for Mrs. Shelby's compassionate act. This kind of discordant realism is Stowe at her best, in my opinion, where the uncritical sentimental scenes such as in the Quaker kitchen are among her weaker moments.)

In any event, Mrs. Shelby comes to do more than express sympathy and shed tears; she vows to buy Tom back as soon as she can "command the money" (167). While Tom and Chloe's reaction is not given, suggesting that they are not pinning too much hope on this promise, Mrs. Shelby proves true to her word and does secure the repurchase of Tom later in the novel. Unfortunately, it is too late.

Chloe has another negative reaction to Mrs. Shelby later in the departure scene. When Haley snaps leg shackles on Tom, Mrs. Shelby asks him to remove them. But Haley says he's already lost five hundred dollars on Eliza's son and that he's running no further risks. Chloe thinks "indignantly," "What else could she spect on him?" (169)—suggesting an exasperation with Mrs. Shelby's naiveté, and further undermining Mrs. Shelby's philosophy of mitigating an evil system through benign treatment, a philosophy she herself has already come to condemn, as we noted earlier, in favor of an abolitionist stance. Chloe retains her dignity throughout the departure, refusing to weep or beg. "I's done *my* tears," she says, "looking grimly at the trader, who was coming up," adding, "I does not feel to cry 'fore dat ar old limb, no how!" (168).

After Haley drives Tom off in his wagon, young Master George, who had been away and not known of the sale, comes galloping up and embraces Tom in a tearful farewell. Tom cautions him against anger and violence and tells him to be a good Christian. George gives Tom a silver dollar to wear around his neck, as a sign of his promise to come and retrieve him. He chides Haley for adding handcuffs to Tom's indignities (Haley does not put them on) and exclaims that he should be ashamed of his profession. But Haley counters that he is no different from George's parents, "'tan't any meaner sellin' on 'em, than 't is buyin'!" (173). George claims that he will do neither when he grows up and announces, "I'm ashamed, this day, that I'm a Kentuckian." Stowe adds sarcastically, "as if he expected the state would be impressed with his opinion" (173). The chapter ends with Tom assuring Haley he has no intention of running off, which, Stowe comments, "seemed rather . . . superfluous" coming from "a man with a great pair of iron fetters on his feet" (174).

As Tom and Haley ride along Stowe engages in one of her favorite exercises, contrasting two characters. In this case the opposition is drawn between their inner thoughts. Stowe observes, "the reflections of two men sitting side by side are a curious thing,—seated on the same seat, having the same eyes, ears, hands and organs of all sorts, and having pass before their eyes the same objects,—it is wonderful what a variety we shall find in these same reflections" (192). Thus, once again we find juxtaposed antithetical worlds—that of the oppressor versus that of the oppressed. Haley is contemplating how much he will get for Tom and how to compose the "gang" of slaves he will assemble to accompany Tom at his sale. He also reflects on how humane he is that he is not forcing Tom to wear handcuffs. Tom, on the other hand, is rehearsing biblical phrases that promise eventual salvation, inspiring him beyond the "blackness of despair" (193).

In order to make up his gang, Haley decides to go to a slave auction in Washington, Kentucky. While he spends the night in a tavern, Tom is lodged in the local jail. The auction takes place the following morning. In *The Key to "Uncle Tom's Cabin"* Stowe indicates that much of the material in this scene was derived from actual documents,[1] but they are brought to life by Stowe's extraordinary visual imagination. Once again, one has the sense of being transposed back in time and participating in the actual texture of nineteenth-century life. "About eleven o'clock . . . a mixed throng was gathered around the court-house steps,—smoking, chewing, spitting, swearing, and cowering. . . . The men and women to be sold sat in a group apart, talking in a low tone to one another" (194).

Haley forces his way into the group, "walked up to [an] old man, pulled his mouth open and looked in, felt of his teeth, made him stand and straighten himself, bend his back, and perform various evolutions to show his muscles; and then passed on to the next, and put him through the same trial" (195). It is here that the elderly woman, Aunt Hagar, is pleading with traders to buy her along with her only remaining son, Albert, but Haley coldly rejects the idea as unprofitable.

When the time comes for Albert to stand on the auction block, "holding fast to her boy," Hagar begs, "Put us two up togedder, togedder,—do please, Mas'r" (196). But the man "gruffly" says "be off . . . you come last," pulling her hands away and pushing the boy toward the block, urging, "Now, darkey, spring" (196). Haley wins the bid for the boy but refuses to take the mother, who is purchased "for a trifle" by a more compassionate man. "The poor victims of the sale . . . gathered around the despairing old mother, whose agony was pitiful to see. 'Couldn't dey leave me one? Mas'r allus said I should have one,—he did,' she repeated over and over, in heart-broken tones" (197). One of the other slaves tells her to "trust in the Lord," but she despairs, "what good will it do" (197). The boy and his mother are then parted forever.

The intense pity of this scene, still powerfully moving, undoubtedly flowed from Stowe's own recent agony over the death of her son Charley, which, as we noted earlier, she herself recognized as a major source of the emotional power of the work. In an 1853 letter Stowe revealed the passionate intensity of her involvement in the novel. "I suffer exquisitely in writing these things. It may be truly said that I write with my heart's blood. Many times in writing 'Uncle Tom's Cabin' I thought my health would fail utterly. . . . This horror, this nightmare abomination! can it be in my country! It lies like lead upon my heart, it shadows my life with sorrow."[2] The intensity of Stowe's feelings clearly stem from her hatred of slavery, but they also, as Anthony Burgess has perceptively remarked, seem to connect to her experience as a bereaved mother. "[N]o amount of abstract, diffused abhorrence of slavery—appropriate to a male writer—could have given *Uncle Tom's Cabin* its peculiar bitterness."[3]

Several similarly painful episodes follow in this chapter, which is entitled "Select Incident of Lawful Trade." The remaining occurrences take place on the Mississippi riverboat *La Belle Riviere,* on which Tom and the other slaves are transported south. Here the juxtaposition between the two worlds, oppressor and oppressed, is dramatically drawn, according to the boat's decks. "Floating gayly down the stream, under a brilliant sky, the stripes and stars of free America waving and fluttering overhead [an obvious irony]. . . . All was full of life, buoyant and rejoicing;—all but Haley's gang, who were stored, with other freight, on the lower deck" (198).

As often in Stowe's public scenes, a discussion about slavery ensues among the white passengers. One woman says it's a disgrace to have such sights as Haley's chained gang in a free country. Another woman says blacks in the south are better off than they would be free. The first woman, however, says regardless of how well they are treated, they still must endure the outrage of forced family separations, which the second woman deflects by saying that blacks do not feel as whites do. The first then objects, "I know they *do* feel, just as keenly,—

even more so, perhaps,—as we do" (199–200). This issue—whether blacks had feelings like whites'—was, as noted, central in the slavery debates of the time.

Stowe takes this occasion to excoriate the standard church position of the period, which was proslavery. A minister chimes in to the discussion, saying, "It's undoubtedly the intention of Providence that the African race should be servants,—kept in a low condition," citing Genesis 9:25, "Cursed be Canaan" (200). Another bystander turns to Haley, saying that this must be a "refreshing" idea for him, but Haley says he knows nothing about scripture, that he "took up the trade just to make a living" (201) and plans to repent, if necessary, later. The bystander sarcastically says that, according to the minister, if Haley had studied his Bible properly he would not have had to worry, since slavery, the minister claims, is sanctioned there (see also 279). Another onlooker pipes up, reminding the group that scripture also says "All things whatsoever ye would that men should do unto you, do ye even so unto them" (201)—which was undoubtedly Stowe's own position.

Several miserable examples of slaves being separated from loved ones follow this discussion. One woman had been betrayed by her master, who told her she was being hired out as a cook in the same tavern as her husband; she finds that she has been sold "down river." The woman, Lucy, has a ten-month-old child, whom Haley sells behind her back. When the boat docks in Louisville, and Lucy runs to the rail, hoping to catch a glimpse of her husband, the child's new owner grabs the infant and races off the boat. Soon after she discovers the loss, the woman commits suicide by jumping overboard.

Stowe comments cynically that Haley's callousness in this incident was not an attribute uniquely inherent in him; rather, it is a state of mind that everyone can develop. Addressing the reader, she says, "His heart was exactly where yours, sir, and mine could be brought, with proper effort and cultivation. The wild look of anguish and utter despair that the woman cast on him might have disturbed one less practiced; but he was used to it. He had seen that same look hundreds of times. You can get used to such things, too, my friend; and it is the great object of recent efforts to make our whole northern community used to them, for the glory of the Union" (208)—another allusion to the Fugitive Slave Law. So Stowe is essentially subscribing here to a theory that in recent times has been called the "banality of evil"[4]—the idea that evil is committed not so much by monsters who are born bad but by ordinary people, just doing their jobs, who become deadened to the suffering around them because they are encouraged by ideology and law to ignore its reality. Thus, Stowe claims, we can all become enculturated to ignore evil and thus permit its existence. Hence its everyday "banality," and hence the cynicism of Stowe's tone in this passage.

In the next several chapters Stowe introduces an entirely new cast of characters, the members of the St. Clare entourage whom Tom happens to meet on the riverboat. Stowe's epic enthusiasm is awakened in the opening descriptions of this second great section of the novel. "The Mississippi!" she exclaims. "What other river of the world bears on its bosom to the ocean the wealth and enterprise of such another country?—a country whose products embrace all between the tropics and the poles! Those turbid waters, hurrying, foaming, tearing along, an apt resemblance of that headlong tide of business which is poured along its wave by a race more vehement and energetic than any the old world ever saw" (226). Here Stowe is speaking as a Jacksonian American, proud of the vitality of the new country. But she adds, "Ah! would that they did not also bear along a more fearful freight,—the tears of the oppressed, the sighs of the helpless" (226–27). From a perch amid the cotton bales on the upper deck Tom surveys the terrain as they enter the deep South. (Haley had come to trust him enough to allow him free run of the boat.) "He saw the distant slaves at their toil; he saw afar their villages of huts gleaming out in long rows on many a plantation, distant from the stately mansions and pleasure-grounds of the master" (228)—a further example of Stowe's panoramic sweep.

Approximately one hundred miles north of New Orleans, we meet little Eva. Her name, Evangeline, the chapter title, is based on the root *evangel,* which means "gospel" and is derived from the Greek *euangelion,* "good news." The nickname Eva, of course, recalls Eve, the primal mother of the human race in Judeo-Christian mythology. Since Eve is traditionally the source of original sin, and since Eva is preternaturally uncorrupt, Stowe seems to be rejecting orthodoxy here (like her father and unlike orthodox Calvinists she did not believe in original sin). Eva's last name, St. Clare, which derives from the Latin *clarus*, "clear," also suggests an unmediated truth or vision.

Eva is not a realistic character; indeed the sections of *Uncle Tom's Cabin* pertaining to little Eva are perhaps the most difficult for the modern reader, influenced by Freudian theories about childhood culpability, to accept. But she must be understood in somewhat allegorical terms. Stowe was, I believe, trying to dramatize sainthood in the character Eva, to show what a purely good, uncorrupt person would be. Like the characters in Dante's *Paradiso* she is the embodiment of a beatific vision, and one simply has to accept her on this level and not apply realistic criteria.

Thus, Eva, who is between five and six years old when we meet her, is described as a flawless paragon. We learn, for example, that "her form was the perfection of childish beauty. . . . There was about it an undulating and aerial grace, such as one might dream of for some mythic and allegorical figure" (230). Here Stowe is clearly cluing the reader in that Eva is to be understood in symbolic terms. "The shape of her head and the turn of her neck and bust was peculiarly noble, and the long golden-brown hair that floated like a cloud around it, the deep spiritual gravity of her violet blue eyes, shaded by heavy fringes of golden brown,—all marked her out from other children, and made every one turn and look after her, as she glided hither and thither on the boat" (230). Unfortunately, the physical descriptions of Eva are fairly characteristic of a sentimentalist type figure, the angelic child, and therefore border on cliché (indeed Eva helped to establish the stereotype). However, in the intensity of her sensitivity to suffering and of her compassion, demonstrated later in the novel, Eva is beyond hackneyed formula, reflecting a profound religious sensibility. "Always dressed in white, she seemed to move like a shadow through all sorts of places, without contacting spot or stain" (231)—symbolically suggesting her inherently incorruptible nature and indicating that she is one of the blessed, one of the elect, a redemptive figure, or as some have suggested, a "feminine Christ."[5] In many respects, strangely, Eva more nearly fits the Roman Catholic figure of the Virgin Mary, who, according to the doctrine of the Immaculate Conception, was the only human being born without original sin. Nevertheless, it is finally within the parameters of Edwardsean Calvinism that we must understand the child.

In his *Treatise Concerning the Religious Affections* Jonathan Edwards explained the character of the blessed: "All who are truly religious are not of this world, they are strangers here, and belong to heaven; they are born from above, heaven is their native country, and the nature which they receive by this heavenly birth, is an heavenly nature, they receive an anointing from above; that principle of true religion which is in them, is a communicator of the religion of heaven, their grace is the dawn of glory; and God fits them for that world by conforming them to it."[6] Eva (as well as Tom) is of this type.

Not surprisingly Tom is drawn to Eva on the boat. "To him she seemed something almost divine . . . he half believed he saw one of the angels stepped out of his New Testament" (231). Often Eva ministers to the slave gang, sighing over their chains and distributing food among them (here as elsewhere in the novel the sharing of food has a sacramental sense, a literal enactment of Holy Communion).

Shortly after Uncle Tom and little Eva introduce themselves, Eva falls overboard just as the boat is starting up and the giant water-wheel beginning its revolution. Tom, "a broad-chested, strong-armed fellow," jumps in immediately and saves her (233). Eva had already told Tom she would ask her father to buy him, and after this St. Clare is willing to do so. He haggles over the price with Haley, with both arguing over the relative value of Tom's attributes, to the extent that Eva, who is standing by, is unsure whether her father is going to conclude the deal. She urges him again saying, "You have money enough, I know. I want him." As critic Spillers points out (see chapter 3), this is one of the few expressions of white female desire in the novel, yet it seems forced to extrapolate sexual interest from Eva's statement. Indeed, Eva and Tom's relationship is wholly asexual, and there seems little point in trying to see it otherwise. (One of Baldwin's criticisms of Tom in fact was that he had been "divested of his sex.") Stowe may indeed have been attempting to debunk the myth of the black rapist through Tom's avuncular relationship with Eva. One critic, Leslie Fiedler, suggests that Stowe was conscious of the issue and was trying "to establish a counter-stereotype to the black rapist" in Simon Legree, a white rapist who preys on black women.[7] In this scene Eva's father asks her jokingly if she wants Tom as a toy. She responds, no, she simply wants "to make him happy," which St. Clare finds "an original reason, certainly" (236) but one that is consistent with her compassionate nature.

Augustine St. Clare is one of the most interesting characters in the novel. While "the gay, pleasure-loving and generous-hearted Southerner" was something of a stock figure in the plantation novels that preceded *Uncle Tom's Cabin,*[8] St. Clare is far from a stereotype. The opening description suggests something of his complexity. "In the large, clear blue eyes, though in form and color exactly similar [to Eva's], there was wanting that misty, dreamy depth of expression; all was clear [reflecting his name, of course], bold, and bright, but with a light wholly of this world: the beautifully cut mouth had a proud and somewhat sarcastic expression, while [he had] an air of free-and-easy superiority. . . . He was listening, with a good-humored, negligent air, half comic, half contemptuous, to Haley, who was very volubly expatiating on the quality of the article for which they were bargaining" (234).

Augustine is of French descent and therefore according to Stowe's racial theories more emotional and poetic than his Anglo-Saxon counterparts (see chapter 6). St. Clare in fact has a somewhat feminine character. As a child "he was remarkable for an extreme and marked sensitiveness of character, more akin to the softness of woman than the ordinary hardness of his own sex. Time, however, overgrew this softness with the rough bark of manhood" (239). Unlike his twin brother, Alfred—another set of antithetical characters—Augustine is "dreamy and inactive" while the former is "active and observing" (334). Where St. Clare is sympathetic with the slaves, refusing to punish them for weighing their cotton sacks with stones and dirt, Alfred is "utterly unmerciful" (334), accusing Augustine of being a "womanish sentimentalist" (342). Where Alfred is his "father's pet" (334), Augustine is his mother's child; he had a "repugnance to the actual business of life" (240) and was instead a "poetical voluptuary" (253).

Augustine suffered a traumatic love affair in his youth that had scarred him for life. Through a mix-up in correspondence, Augustine came to believe he had been jilted by his northern fiancée, the great love of his life. On the rebound he marries "the reigning belle of the season," discovering too late that his former lover still loved him and had been the victim of a fraudulent scheme to break off their engagement. Undermined by his secret passion for another, the relationship with his wife soon founders.

One other aspect of Augustine's character should be mentioned here, his lazy extravagance. Hardly an efficient manager, he runs a lax undisciplined estate and is "indolent and careless of money" (305). Tom, soon installed as manager of the St. Clare estate in New Orleans but accustomed to managing the Shelby plantation with orderly efficiency, is shocked at "the wasteful expenditure of the establishment" (305) and casts a critical eye on St. Clare's happy-go-lucky irresponsibility (306). A more negative version of Augustine is his wife, Marie, who is similarly "indolent and childish, unsystematic and improvident" (309). Unlike her northern counterpart, Mrs. Shelby—against whom she is set up antithetically—Marie mismanages and neglects her estate. Mrs. Shelby, by contrast, is able to "bring into harmonious and systematic order, the various members of their small estate,—to regulate their peculiarities, and so balance and compensate the deficiencies of one by the excess of another, as to produce a harmonious and orderly system" (309)—another description of Stowe's ideal of a well-run, just system. Here too we may note that the St. Clare estate is a kind of way station on Stowe's symbolic map between the orderly rule seen in northern locations and the extreme disorder and chaos of the Legree plantation.

The St. Clare province is one of indolent sensuality. That impression is established in Stowe's description of the mansion when the entourage arrives at the estate grounds. The architecture is "an odd mixture of Spanish and French . . . built in the Moorish fashion" (252) and therefore expressive of the passionate exuberance of those races. The "Moorish arches, slender pillars, and arabesque ornaments, carried the mind, as in dream, to . . . oriental romance." A fountain in the courtyard, "pellucid as crystal, was alive with myriads of gold and silver fishes, twinkling and darting through it like so many jewels." The "green velvet" grounds are dotted by orange trees, "pomegranate trees, with their glossy leaves and flame-colored flowers, dark-leaved Arabian jessamines . . . geraniums, luxuriant roses . . . golden jessamines, lemon-scented verbenum." In short, "the appearance of the place was luxurious and romantic" (253).

Miss Ophelia, Augustine's Yankee cousin, thinks it looks "heathenish," while Tom is attracted to its rich splendor, though, as noted, he is soon critical of its luxury. One has the impression that in this Louisiana environment we are right at the edge of the rational world; the irrational, the sensual, and evil are barely held in check. At the same time there is a pleasant easygoing indulgence about the place that would not be possible in northern regions, controlled as they are by "the colder and more correct white [Anglo-Saxon] race" (253).

Marie, next to Simon Legree the most despicable character in the novel, bears many of the earmarks of the selfish "belle" type, a stock figure in women's literature of the period, treated by Stowe in several of her early stories, including her first published story, "Isabelle and Her Sister Kate, and Their Cousin" (1834).[9] Like them Marie's entire purpose in life is one of self-absorbed, narcissistic ornamentation. Her every caprice has been catered to since infancy, and she is incapable of empathy or love. Stowe does complicate her psychology somewhat by having her dimly aware of her husband's disaffection. Early in their marriage he is given to headaches and therefore "didn't enjoy going into company with her." It seemed "odd" to her "to go so much alone, when they were just married" (242). So she develops a kind of vague jealousy and degenerates into a neurasthenic hypochondriac, "a yellow faded, sickly woman, whose time was divided among a variety of fanciful diseases, and who considered herself, in every sense, the most ill-used and suffering person in existence" (243). We have noted how she contrasts to the active, healthy Mrs. Shelby; she is also drawn in counterpoint to her servant Mammy. When Eva arrives home after her long absence, Marie brushes her aside, saying she has a headache, where Mammy, the true mother, embraces her with great emotion (255). As one might expect, Marie's attitude toward the slaves is harsh, unfeeling, and exacting.

Ophelia is another remarkable character, whose originality has not been fully appreciated. She is one of the first intellectual women in literature, entirely able to hold her own in vigorous debates with St. Clare over slavery. Some have suggested that as a moralistic Yankee she is Stowe's own comical, critical self-portrait. A forty-five-year-old spinster, Ophelia grew up in a "cool," orderly New England village, another representation of Stowe's utopian society. A typical farmhouse in such villages, Stowe remarks, exudes an "air of order and stillness, of perpetuity and unchanging repose. Nothing lost, or out of order; not a picket loose in the fence, not a particle of litter in the . . . yard." There were no servants; all the work was done effortlessly and gracefully by the housewife and her daughters (244–45), in contrast to the St. Clare mansion.

As one might expect, coming from such a background, Ophelia "was a living impersonation of order, method, and exactness. . . . The great sin of sins, in her eyes,—the sum of all evils,—was expressed by one very common and important word in her vocabulary—'shiftlessness' " (247). By this she meant indolent purposelessness: "people who did nothing, or who did not know exactly what they were going to do, or who did not take the most direct way to accomplish what they set their hands to, were objects of her entire contempt" (247).

Ophelia "had a clear, strong, active mind, was well and thoroughly read" (248) and is driven by a "dominant and all-absorbing" conscience, "the granite formation" in New England women. She is "the absolute bond-slave of the '*ought*' " and is rigidly willful. "Once make her certain that the 'path of duty'. . . lay in any given direction . . . fire and water could not keep her from it" (248). Despite the uncompromising austerity of Ophelia's character, she has a sense of humor and a warm heart. Stowe realizes the sharp contrast she has drawn between the northern and southern cousins, Ophelia and Augustine, and asks, "how in the world can Miss Ophelia get along with Augustine St. Clare, gay, unpunctual, unpractical, skeptical,—in short,—walking with impudent and nonchalant freedom over every one of her most cherished habits and opinions?" The answer is surprising: "To tell the truth, then, Ophelia loved him. . . . [She] laughed at his jokes, and forebore with his failings" (248–49). She also loves little Eva, and it is for this reason she has agreed to come south: to help manage the St. Clare menage in the vacuum of Marie's negligence and to help educate Eva.

Ophelia, however, despite her rectitude has a lot to learn. In theory she disapproves of slavery, but in physical terms she is repelled by blacks, a feeling she only gradually overcomes. When she protests that Eva's sitting on Tom's knee is "dreadful," St. Clare takes the occasion to criticize northern hypocrisy: "You loathe them as you would a snake or a toad, yet you are indignant at their wrongs. You would not have them abused; but you don't want to have anything to do with them yourselves. You would send them to Africa, out of your sight and smell" (273; see also 425). Ophelia acknowledges that St. Clare may be right. He says further that southerners, while they hardly have a corner on virtue, at least are comfortable with blacks physically. "[C]ustom with us does what Christianity ought to do,—obliterates the feeling of personal prejudice" (273). St. Clare's attitude toward the slaves, while lackadaisical and indulgent, is nevertheless condescending. He refers to Tom as "boy" (238) and on his return distributes "small pieces of change" among the Negroes, calling them "good boys and girls" (256).

Several of the blacks in the St. Clare household are fully developed characters. Adolph, the chief butler, is a "highly-dressed young mulatto" (254) and something of a "dandy" (256). "As careless and extravagant as his master" (305), Adolph had managed to line his own pocket while in charge of the St. Clare finances. "Thoughtless and self-indulgent, and unrestrained by a master who found it easier to indulge than to regulate, he had fallen into an absolute confusion as to *meum tuum* with regard to himself and his master, which sometimes troubled even St. Clare" (306). Adolph's behavior is an example of the problematic status of the St. Clare estate on Stowe's moral spectrum. His venalities are not serious enough to be considered wholly evil or wrong, yet the casual nonchalance that allows such indulgence to continue without check can lead to a tolerance of more serious wrongdoing. Indeed, St. Clare's negligence and irresponsibility result in Tom's eventual sale to Legree, a much greater evil. So Tom's dismay at Adolph's embezzlement and St. Clare's lazy indulgence of it suggests a prophetic awareness of where such venial sins might lead. (St. Clare does, however, gradually replace Adolph with Tom, who is, of course, much more trustworthy and competent, as the primary manager of the purse.)

Another major black character is Mammy. Also mulatto, she habitually wears a "high red and yellow turban" (259) and generally runs the domestic scene. As Marie's personal servant, she is relentlessly oppressed. Separated for years from her own husband and two children, who are at Marie's father's plantation, Mammy is required to wait on Marie day and night. When Eva notices how exhausted Mammy has become, she asks if she can relieve her in attending Marie one night, so Mammy can get some rest. But Marie dismisses Mammy's complaints as self-indulgent (263). During Eva's illness Marie, indulging in her own neurotic hysteria, keeps Mammy in such close attendance she has little time for Eva (398). "Twenty times in a night, Mammy would be roused to rub [Marie's] feet, to bathe her head, to find her pocket-handkerchief, to see what the noise was in Eva's room . . . ; and, in the daytime, when she longed to have some share in the nursing of her pet [Eva], Marie seemed unusually ingenious in keeping her busy" (423).

The kitchen in the St. Clare estate is the province of Dinah, another memorable character. As a cook she was "a self-taught genius, and like geniuses in general, was positive, opinionated and erratic" (310). Like Aunt Chloe, she "ruled supreme" by dint of her "impregnable" self-confidence, such that even Marie had long since ceased trying to control her (310). Before she began preparations for a meal Dinah smoked "a short, stumpy pipe, to which she was much addicted" and sat on the kitchen floor waiting for inspiration. Dinah's kitchen is a paradigm of chaotic disorder, of Ophelia's "shiftlessness." Dishes are never washed; staples are scattered at random in drawers with an odd assortment of other items, including Dinah's hair grease, soiled Madras handkerchiefs, a couple of old shoes, some twine, and darning needles (313); "the rolling-pin is under her bed, and the nutmeg-grater in her pocket with her tobacco" (317). In short, the kitchen "looked as if it had been arranged by a hurricane blowing through it" (311).

Like Adolph's venality, Dinah's disorder symbolizes the tenuous moral state of the St. Clare world. In a perceptive article Gillian Brown suggests that Dinah's kitchen represents the intrusion of capitalist marketplace behavior into the planned domestic economy, which Stowe saw as antithetical. "[T]he variable state of Dinah's kitchen exhibits the antithesis of domestic economy—the fluctuating marketplace. . . . Exponents of domesticity defined the home as a peaceful order in contrast to the disorder and fluctuations occasioned by competitive economic activity in the marketplace," which is ruled by irrational whim. An even more serious erosion of domestic order, of course, is seen at the Legree plantation, a whimsical, irrational masculine tyranny that exemplifies unbridled capitalism at its worst.[10]

One character introduced in the St. Clare section of the novel who prefigures the degeneration of the Legree world is Prue, a slave on a neighboring plantation. Her story is probably the most shocking yet presented in the work and her fate the most horrible. Prue has been kept as a "breeder," which means that her job is to produce children as quickly as possible, who are then sold by speculators immediately. Finally she is bought by a master who allows her to keep one of her children, but Prue becomes ill and loses her milk. The mistress on the plantation refuses to allow her to obtain other milk for the infant, who thus starves. Nor will she allow Prue to stay with the child, whom she must leave alone at night in a garret, while she attends the mistress. The baby then cries itself to death alone.

After the child's death, Prue takes to drinking to dull her pain and in order to support her habit begins stealing the master's money, for which she is regularly beaten. Dinah comments that "her back's a far sight now,—she can't never get a dress together over it" (321). Tom tries to introduce her to Christianity and promises her she will find peace in heaven, but Prue comments bitterly that she would "rather go to torment" if "white folks" like her owners are to be found in heaven (324). Even the other slaves treat Prue with contempt because of her thievery and drinking; she has become a despised outcast. Only Tom and Eva seem to feel compassion for her, but Prue is beyond help. Discovered stealing one last time, she is beaten to death. "[T]hey had her down cellar,—and then they left her all day,—and I hearn 'em saying that the *flies had got to her,*—and *she's dead!*" (326). The shocking cruelty and evil seen in Prue's story portend events to come.

9

Discussions, Death, and Dissolution

In the middle of the chapters about the St. Clare estate, Stowe interposes a chapter (17) that brings us up to date on George and Eliza's fate. In one of the most exciting episodes in the novel, the Harrises flee further north to escape the slave catchers, Loker and Marks, who are fast closing in. One of the Quakers, Phineas Fletcher, a Dickensian character, redheaded, "tall and lathy" (285), happens to overhear the slave catchers' plans while stopping overnight in a tavern. He learns that they have discovered George and Eliza's whereabouts and are preparing to make their capture. Phineas quickly makes his way to the Halliday home to warn the fugitives, and soon all are on the next leg of their escape (also there are Jim, the man who had earlier posed as George's servant, and his mother, whom he had in the meantime rescued from slavery). Both Jim and George are armed, which the Quakers disapprove of but understand.

At one point in the pursuit the slave catchers come within sight, and a breathless chase ensues. Phineas knows of a secret hiding place in a rocky range, and the fugitives manage to scurry to cover just as the catchers move in. Loker and Marks's posse includes two constables and "such rowdies at the last tavern as could be engaged by a little bravery to go and help the fun of trapping a set of niggers" (297).

In a dramatic scene George, standing on a rock, confronts his pursuers, saying "I am George Harris. . . . I'm a free man. . . . We have arms to defend ourselves, and we mean to do it" (298). Stowe calls this "his declaration of independence" (298) and compares his stand to that of the uprising of Hungarian youth against the Austro-Hungarian empire in the Revolution of 1848. (Stowe later alludes to the voluntary emancipation of the serfs by the Hungarian nobles—an important result of the 1848 revolution—as a possible model for the emancipation of the American slaves [451–52].) Marks's response to George's speech is to shoot at him while Loker leads the charge up the rock. George wounds him, which dissuades the rest of the posse, who quickly retreat, abandoning Loker. The Quaker party then safely deposits the Harrises (and Loker) in the next way station on the underground railway.

Stowe drops the thread of the Harris narrative here, picking it up again only late in the novel (chapter 37). There we learn that the Harrises were left in the care of Quaker Aunt Dorcas, a peaceable, maternal woman under whose care Loker begins to repent. He advises the Harrises about slave-catcher tactics and decides to abandon his own trade. Following Loker's suggestion, George, Eliza, and Harry don disguises for the final stage of their journey, a trip across Lake Erie to Canada. Eliza dresses as a man and Harry as a girl. There is a certain comic aspect to Eliza's attempt to play the part: "I must stamp, and take long steps, and try to look saucy" (547). Their camouflage works, and under the shepherding of another Quaker, Mrs. Smyth, they arrive finally in Canada.

Meanwhile, weightier events are happening farther south. A substantial portion of the St. Clare section of the novel is devoted to lengthy discussions and debates between St. Clare and other characters, principally Ophelia and his brother Alfred. These dialectical exchanges are a brilliant tour de force.

Ophelia is surprised to learn, soon after arriving in New Orleans, that St. Clare thinks slavery is an evil system but nevertheless continues to own slaves. He does so not because he thinks it is right but because he can see no alternative. In response to Ophelia's challenging questions, St. Clare reveals his theory about slavery. As already noted, it is essentially a Marxist theory of materialist determinism. People's principal motivation is economic, and ideological justifications follow. "Planters, who have money to make by it,—clergymen, who have planters to please,—politicians, who want to rule by it,— . . . warp and bend language and ethics to a degree that shall astonish the world" (331).

While there is no evidence that Stowe had read Marx or Engels, it seems likely, given her acute interest in contemporary affairs, that she was at least familiar with some of their ideas. *The Communist Manifesto*, issued in German in 1848, had been translated into English by 1850. The first U.S. publication was not until 1872, however (ironically, in *Woodhull and Claflin's Weekly*, the organ of Stowe's archenemy of the 1870s, Victoria Woodhull). Most critics seem to feel, however, that St. Clare's theories derive from Orestes Brownson, an American thinker, who several years before *The Communist Manifesto* advocated the abolition of "hereditary property" to end "economic exploitation," which he saw as the root of social evil. He also believed the injustices of slavery stemmed not from individual slaveholders but from the system itself. Brownson's ideas were published in a Cincinnati journal, *Western Messenger*, in 1839–41, while Stowe was there, so it is likely she knew of them firsthand.[1]

St. Clare's elaboration of these ideas casts them in somewhat cynical terms, seeing slavery's perpetuation finally as an issue of power. "Strip it of all its ornament . . . and what is it? Why, because my brother Quashy is ignorant and weak, and I am intelligent and strong. . . . Because I don't like work, Quashy shall work, Quashy shall earn money, and I will spend it" (331). St. Clare recognizes that "the *thing itself* is the essence of all abuse" and this largely because it allows absolute power to accrue to one individual, the slaveholder. "[E]very brutal, disgusting, mean, low-lived fellow . . . [is] allowed by our laws to become absolute despot of as many men, women and children, as he could cheat, steal, or gamble money enough to buy" (332).

Earlier Ophelia asked in response to the news of Prue's beating whether there weren't "*selectmen,* or anybody, to interfere and look after such matters?" (327). St. Clare says that there are no such laws because it is assumed that "the *property* interest is a sufficient guard in such cases" (327), meaning that most owners do not want to seriously damage their property by inflicting severe physical harm and that in any event, since Prue was a thief and drunkard, the general sentiment is that she deserves her punishment. When Ophelia exclaims that this is "perfectly outrageous . . . horrid" (327), Augustine says that there is nothing he can do about it: "The best we can do is to shut our eyes and ears" (328)—an essentially apathetic response to the problem of evil, exemplified in the brutal treatment of Prue.

The other aspect of St. Clare's theory that has a peculiarly Marxist ring is the analogy he draws between the condition of the slaves and that of the workers or proletariat under capitalist industrialism. "Look at the high and the low all the world over, and it's the same story,—the lower class used up, body, soul, and spirit, for the good of the upper. It is so in England; it is so everywhere" (319).

St. Clare's brother Alfred expresses a similar idea, but from the point of view of the capitalist. He argues that the southern planter is "only doing in another form, what the English aristocracy and capitalists are doing by the lower classes"—namely, Augustine adds, "*appropriating* them, body and bone, soul and spirit, to their use and convenience" (340). Ophelia objects to the analogy: "The English laborer is not sold, traded, parted from his family, whipped." But St. Clare retorts, "He is as much at the will of his employer as if he were sold to him. The slave-owner can whip his refractory slave to death,—the capitalist can starve him to death. As to family security, it's hard to say which is the worst,—to have one's children sold, or see them starve to death at home" (341). Indeed, he claims, American slaves are probably better off than the lower classes in England (341).

St. Clare wholly recognizes, however, the debilitating effect of slavery, especially the hard, relentless toil inflicted on the field hands. "Tell me that any man living wants to work all his days, from daydawn till dark, under the constant eye of a master, . . . on the same, dreary, monotonous, unchanging toil . . . !" (339–40). But here too St. Clare's comment could well be applied to the alienated labor of the factory worker.

St. Clare anticipates a worldwide revolution of the masses—again like that called for in *The Communist Manifesto*. "[T]here is a mustering among the masses the world over; and there is a *dies irae* coming on, sooner or later. The same thing is working in Europe, in England, and in this country" (344). In a later conversation with his brother Alfred, Augustine predicts again, "the masses are to rise, and the under class become the upper one," referring to the French Revolution and an 1804 revolution in Haiti in which black slaves rose up and killed whites on the island (392).

In her conclusion to the novel Stowe predicts a violent "last convulsion." "This is an age . . . when nations are trembling and convulsed. A mighty influence is abroad" (629). She warns that unless peaceful steps are taken to alleviate injustice and end slavery there will be a violent cataclysm. Her notion appears to combine an apocalyptic vision of the last judgment with that of a political revolution, an uprising of the slaves. While her position in *Uncle Tom's Cabin* remained one of Christian nonresistance, during the decade of the 1850s Stowe grew to support violence and insurrection as a tactic (she applauded John Brown's raid on Harper's Ferry in 1859, for example), and she came to see the Civil War as an expression of God's wrath, an instrument of divine retribution, but also as an aspect of a worldwide political rebellion of the masses. As early as *Dred* (1856), her next novel after *Uncle Tom's Cabin*, Stowe concluded that peaceful persuasion was not enough; only violent revolution would end slavery. "The only force," she felt by this time, that "could alter such a [capitalist] society would come from the violent reaction of revolutionary groups alienated by a materialist and repressive social order."[2]

Alfred, Augustine's antithetical brother, takes the opposite point of view, that of the upper classes. He argues for a stratified society with a servant class built in at the bottom to provide for the needs of the rich at the top. "[T]here can be no high civilization without enslavement of the masses. . . . There must be . . . a lower class, given up to physical toil and confined to an animal nature; and a higher one [which] thereby acquires leisure and wealth for a more expanded intelligence and improvement" (340). His theory is also racist. "The Anglo-Saxon is the dominant race of the world, and *is to be so*" (392). "We've got the power. This subject race . . . is down and shall *stay* down!" (393). Alfred's ideas derive somewhat from his father, who believed "the negro . . . as an intermediate link between man and animals" (335) and treated his five hundred slave laborers accordingly.

Augustine, encouraged by his mother, came to believe, however, that Negroes were human beings who had immortal souls and therefore found the brutality of his father's plantation intolerable. He left its management to Alfred and moved to the family mansion in New Orleans at an early age. Ophelia wonders, however, why given his sentiments he has not freed his slaves. St. Clare offers a number of reasons but in the end simply appears to be congenitally unable to act. In this he resembles his mother, who is probably the most pathetic example of the morally sensitive but ineffectual white women in the novel; she contrasts markedly with the white wives further north (Mrs. Bird and Mrs. Shelby) who are more influential on their insensitive husbands or who at least do not give up.

But St. Clare says he "wasn't up to" freeing his slaves: "To hold them as tools for money-making, I could not;—have them to help spend money, you know, didn't look quite so ugly to me. Some of them were old house-servants, to whom I was much attached. . . . All were well satisfied to be as they were" (343). A more cogent reason is given later on: "suppose we should rise up tomorrow and emancipate, who would educate these millions, and teach them how to use their freedom?" (452). At the end of the novel Master George Shelby, who has replaced his father as the owner of Shelby plantation, responds in effect to St. Clare's waffling by liberating his slaves but allowing them to stay on the plantation as paid laborers and providing them with an education (616).

But while St. Clare had early felt "vague, indistinct yearning to be a sort of emancipator" (343), he soon decides, "I can't turn knight-errant, and undertake to redress every individual case of wrong"

mand, education, physical and moral eminence; the Afric, born of ages of oppression, submission, ignorance, toil and vice!" (362).

Stowe's conception of Topsy, who is ultimately educated to behave in a moral, civilized way (she eventually becomes a missionary), presents the strongest case against Stowe being a racist in the modern sense. As Mary Church Terrell, a turn-of-the-century black leader, remarked in her defense of Stowe against charges of racism, "The faults and weaknesses of character upon which [the ex-slave's] detractors and ex-masters have always dwelt with so much pleasure were attributed by Mrs. Stowe to his environment rather than to any inherent racial depravity, as certain near-philosophers would have us believe."[3]

Topsy and Eva start as another set of antithetical characters, but Eva's kind and loving treatment gradually draws Topsy into the human fold. At first, however, Topsy is too cynical to believe Eva when she says she would "rather give [Topsy] anything of [hers], than have [her] steal it." Stowe comments, "it was the first word of kindness the child had ever heard in her life . . . [but] the ear that has never heard anything but abuse is strangely incredulous of anything so heavenly as kindness; and Topsy only thought Eva's speech something funny and inexplicable,—she did not believe it" (362). Like the abused child today Topsy's feelings are frozen (she tells Eva "Dunno nothing 'bout love" [407]), and it is only through prolonged and repeated gestures of caring that Eva is able to win her confidence and heal her "broken heart."[4]

Topsy has also internalized a sense of her own inferiority—possibly the most grievous aspect of her benighted experience. When Ophelia asks her why she persists in "raising Cain," Topsy replies, "I dunno, Missis,—I spects cause I's so wicked!" She says the only way to get her to behave is to whip her—here the oppressed taking on the point of view of the oppressor, but Ophelia says she does not want to. Topsy explains, "Laws, Missis, I's used to whippin'; I spects it's good for me." When Ophelia obliges, Topsy ridicules the mildness of the beating to her peers, saying, "Law, Miss Feely whip!—wouldn't kill a skeeter, her whippins. Oughter see how old Mas'r made the flesh fly; old Mas'r know'd how!" Topsy, in fact, comes to take pride in her incorrigible "wickedness," bragging about it to the other slaves. "I's so awful wicked there can't nobody do nothin' with me. . . . I spects I's the wickedest critter in the world" (367).

Later, when St. Clare asks her why she persists in her mischief, Topsy again responds, "Spects it's my wicked heart," explaining that she's a hopeless case because she's "a nigger." "I's so wicked! Laws! I's nothin but a nigger, no ways!" (408). In commenting on this passage in *The Key to "Uncle Tom's Cabin"* Stowe reveals a strikingly modern awareness that Topsy exemplifies the problem of internalized racism— what happens when blacks or other oppressed groups begin to believe the doctrine of inferiority held about them by the dominant, oppressor class. "[I]nscribed on the seal which keeps the great stone over the sepulchre of the African mind . . . is this—which was so truly said by poor Topsy—'NOTHING BUT A NIGGER!' " Stowe notes that black children excel in education until they realize "that society had no place to offer them for which anything more would be requisite than the rudest and most elementary knowledge." They thus lose interest in learning.[5]

In the novel we further discover that Topsy thinks she is unlovable because she is black. "If I could be skinned, and come white, I'd try then," she observes. Eva protests, "But people can love you, if you are black, Topsy" (409), to which Topsy gives "a short, blunt laugh," saying Ophelia "can't bar me, 'cause I'm a nigger!—she'd 's soon have a toad touch her! There can't nobody love niggers, and niggers can't do nothin'!" (409).

Ophelia afterward acknowledges, "I've always had a prejudice against negroes . . . and it's a fact, I never could bear to have that child touch me; but, I don't think she knew it" (410). St. Clare astutely observes that all her efforts to educate Topsy will be for naught as long as the child senses "that feeling of repugnance remains in the heart" (410), but Ophelia is unsure how to overcome her feelings. When St. Clare suggests Eva as a model of one who is able to love Topsy uncondi- tionally, Ophelia protests that Eva is "Christ-like" (411).

Meanwhile Eva has exclaimed in "a sudden burst of feeling," "O, Topsy, poor child, *I* love you!" "laying her little thin, white hand on

Topsy's shoulder," "I love you . . . because you've been a poor, abused child! I love you and I want you to be good" (409). Eva's love and faith in Topsy (she claims, despite her mother's scoffing, that Topsy has an immortal soul [415]) is eventually redemptive, and in the wake of Eva's death Ophelia experiences a kind of conversion (a change of heart) that enables her to overcome her earlier feelings of aversion (443). Ultimately, she adopts Topsy and takes her back north to receive a full education.

The next several chapters (22–26) deal with Eva's deteriorating health and death, but we first return briefly to Kentucky (chapter 21) to the Shelby plantation where we learn that Mrs. Shelby and Aunt Chloe are actively working to raise enough money to repurchase Tom. Mr. Shelby clearly has been mismanaging their finances, but when Mrs. Shelby suggests ways they could recoup their losses—selling the horses or one of their other farms—Shelby ridicules her, saying women "don't understand business" (372). Stowe rejects Shelby's sexist assumption by noting that Mrs. Shelby "had a clear, energetic, practical mind, and a force of character every way superior to that of her husband" (372). Thus, she would have been quite "capable of managing," a thesis that is proven later when she takes over the management of the estate after Shelby's death and competently straightens out their financial mess (587). Mrs. Shelby thus exemplifies Stowe's feminism.

In the meantime Mrs. Shelby vows to take in music students to raise the money, which Mr. Shelby sees as degrading, and Chloe is allowed to hire herself out to a confectionery in Louisville where she can expect to make $208 a year, at which rate she would have enough to buy Tom back in four to five years. Uncle Tom's cabin is to be closed up for the duration. In this plan Chloe and Mrs. Shelby collaborate, another attempt by women to overcome the intransigent capitalist venality of a white male. Meanwhile, events are transpiring farther south that will negate their plans.

As the summer heat intensifies, the St. Clare household moves to the family villa on Lake Pontchartrain, where Eva's dying and death occur. In her final weeks Eva's character as a salvific or Christ figure is accentuated. Her relationship with Tom intensifies. The two share their utopian intuitions of a blessed afterlife, reading appropriate passages from Revelations and Prophesies and singing Methodist hymns about "*Canaan's Shore*" and "*the new Jerusalem*" (381). Eva's appearance becomes increasingly angelic: "the glow of evening lit her golden hair and flushed cheek with a kind of unearthly radiance" (382). She expresses a "strange unworldly wisdom" (385), and her "whole heart and soul seemed absorbed in works of love and kindness" (385).

She teaches the slaves to read the Bible (385); she rescues Dodo, a young slave boy, from the cruel treatment of his master, Henrique, her cousin (388–90), and counsels the latter to love Dodo "and be kind to him, for my sake!" (396). And, as noted, she extends a loving hand to Topsy.

As death nears, her sacrificial purpose becomes clear. She says she longs to "bless and save" the slaves, telling Tom, "I can understand why Jesus *wanted* to die for us. . . . I've felt that I would be glad to die, if my dying would stop all this misery. I *would* die for them, Tom, if I could" (401). Mammy calls her a "dear, little, blessed lamb!" (401). By this time "there was a kind of glory behind [Eva], as she came forward in her white dress, with her golden hair and glowing cheeks, her eyes unnaturally bright . . . [expressing] a kind of beauty so intense, so fragile, that we cannot bear to look at it" (401). In this state Eva asks her father to free the slaves and makes him promise, in particular, that he will manumit Uncle Tom after her death (404).

The death scene itself is cast in images of red and white—traditionally symbols of the heart, *caritas,* and purity, respectively. The curtains in Eva's bedroom are rose and white; the floor matting is bordered with red rosebuds; the centerpiece holds red roses; an alabaster bracket hangs over the bed; the writing table is similarly alabaster; a vase is in the shape of a white lily (412–13). Topsy brings her a bouquet consisting of a scarlet geranium and a white japonica, and Eva's coloring is similarly described as "crimson cheeks contrasting . . . with the intense whiteness of her complexion" (418). One of Eva's final gestures is her address to an assembly of the slaves—a scene well etched in the American popular mind. Eva's message is simple: "I sent for you all, my dear friends . . . because I love you. I love you all."

She assures them that if they are good Christians, they will be saved (here again Stowe parts company with orthodox Calvinism by connecting salvation with good works). "I want you to remember that there is a beautiful world, where Jesus is. I am going there, and you can go there. It is for you, as much as me" (418). She proceeds then to give them each a curl of her hair as a token of her love and faith that she will see them all in heaven (419). Through the final hours Tom's compassion intensifies; he never leaves Eva's side and often carries her about. St. Clare, who is devastated by Eva's dying, also leans on Tom in the last moments. When she finally dies, "a bright, a glorious smile passed over her face, and she said, brokenly,—'O! love,—joy,—peace!' " Thus, Stowe exclaims, she "passed from death into life!" (428)—the ultimate dialectical transition in *Uncle Tom's Cabin.*

Modern critics have for the most part responded to Eva's death, as Tompkins remarks, with "condescending irony." In its intense religiosity and hyperbolic sentimentalism, it is certainly alien to modern secular tastes. Nevertheless, even the most hard-boiled reader must concede that the scene still has a strangely moving effect. Ann Douglas, however, regards the death of little Eva as "Christianity beginning to function as camp"—that is, like the mass cultural distractions of the consumerist twentieth century, it functions only to obfuscate rather than alleviate evil. Douglas maintains that Eva's "beautiful death . . . in no way hinders the working" of slavery, but this is not entirely correct. Eva's dying and death do have a redemptive effect on several characters, moving them toward the "change of heart" that Stowe felt was an essential prerequisite to the mitigation of evil behavior. Two central characters—Ophelia and Topsy—are transformed by Eva's death.

Jane Tompkins's understanding of Eva's death is the more perceptive, in my view. "Stories like the death of little Eva are compelling for the same reason that the story of Christ's death is compelling; they enact a philosophy, as much political as religious, in which the pure and powerless die to save the powerful and corrupt, and thereby show themselves more powerful than those they save. They enact, in short, a *theory* of power . . . [in which] social action is made dependent on the action taking place in individual hearts."[6]

In direct political terms, however, Eva's dying has little effect—largely because in order to be transformed into action her dying requests had to be mediated by a white male, St. Clare, whose ineffectual dalliance negates whatever effect they might have had. St. Clare is killed in a barroom fight before he has acted to free Tom legally or to make any similar provision for the other slaves. After St. Clare's death, the power shifts to Marie, whose heartless attitudes have not been moderated by her daughter's death. In fact, no longer checked by her husband's and daughter's restraints she becomes another example of how the absolute power of the slaveholder corrupts. Within two weeks of St. Clare's death she begins to send some of her slaves to a "whipping establishment" for discipline. It is a place where "women and young girls" are given over to "the lowest of men . . . to be subjected to brutal exposure and shameful correction" (460). Despite Ophelia's protests, the practice continues. A few days later Marie decides to sell most of her slaves. Once again, Ophelia's pleas that she respect Eva's dying wishes that the slaves—especially Tom—be freed fall on deaf ears. Tom is bitterly disappointed, having jubilantly anticipated his freedom earlier when St. Clare initiated the legal proceedings for his manumission (453–54), but tries to accept his fate with Christian resignation (463).

Within days then after his master's death Tom and several of the other slaves find themselves bound for a slave warehouse in New Orleans, where they are to await sale. Thus begins the final segment of *Uncle Tom's Cabin.*

10

Inferno: The Legree Plantation

Uncle Tom moves to center stage in this last, direful section of the novel. It centrally concerns his passage to an inferno on earth, the Legree plantation, where he lives in a hut that is also called a "cabin"—a fact critics seem to have overlooked. Instead of the cozy home he shared with Chloe and his children farther north, however, Uncle Tom's cabin on the Legree plantation is "forlorn, brutal, forsaken," an empty room furnished only with "a heap of straw, foul with dirt, spread confusedly" (494), which adds a grim inflection to the title. The climax of the novel is the confrontation between Tom and Legree, representing two weighty antithetical principles, goodness and evil, the Christ and the Antichrist. As one critic has pointed out, Uncle Tom is the first Christ figure in American literature.[1]

The section opens in the Louisiana slave warehouse where Tom and several other St. Clare slaves are awaiting sale. As in the earlier slave auctions, this episode evokes Stowe's bitterest sarcasm. Slave warehouses, she remarks, are not the hell holes one might expect; "no, innocent friend; in these days men have learned the art of sinning expertly and genteelly so as not to shock the eyes and senses of respectable society" (467). As property, slaves awaiting sale are well treated and well fed. The appearance of propriety makes the underlying reality all the more horrible.

In this part of the narrative Stowe shows more examples of slaves who have been corrupted and morally destroyed by the system. These characters are the true "Uncle Tom's" of the novel in that they behave in the collaborative, obsequious way that has unfortunately and, as we have seen, erroneously become attached to the name *Uncle Tom*. The first of these is Sambo, who works for the slave keeper Skeggs to keep the warehouse in a state of forced cheer by performing "tricks of low buffoonery" (468). Stowe observes, "the dealers in human article make scrupulous and systematic efforts to promote noisy mirth among them, as a means of drowning reflection, and rendering them insensible to their condition" (468). Several of the slaves on the Legree plantation similarly act collusively as henchmen for their master.

As in the earlier auction Stowe proceeds through a painful catalog of the slaves awaiting sale: there is a ten-year-old girl whose mother had been sold the day before, an elderly woman, and a mother and her fifteen-year-old daughter, Susan and Emmeline, the latter of whom figures prominently in the remainder of the narrative. Both are well-educated Christians, and they fear that they will be separated and that Emmeline will be sold into sexual slavery.

Uncle Tom's antagonist, Simon Legree, a potential buyer, is introduced shortly before the sale commences. He is "a short, broad, muscular man, in a checked shirt considerably open at the bosom, and pantaloons much the worse for dirt and wear" (477). Here, as elsewhere, Stowe uses metonymic details to express the man's inner character. "His round, bullet head, large, light-gray eyes, with their shaggy, sandy eyebrows, and stiff, wiry, sun-burned hair, were rather unprepossessing . . . his large, coarse mouth was distended with tobacco . . . his hands were immensely large, hairy, sun-burned, freckled, and very dirty, and garnished with long nails, in a very foul condition" (477). Tom feels "an immediate and revolting horror" at his sight. "He seized Tom by the jaw, and pulled open his mouth to inspect his teeth" (477). In a similarly repulsive gesture he sizes Emmeline up physically, appraising her worth as a sexual commodity. "He put out his heavy dirty hand, and drew the girl towards him; passed it over her neck and bust, felt her arms, looked at her teeth" (477).

The name *Simon* has a long tradition in Western literature. In Acts 8:9–11, 18–23, it is the name of Simon Magus, who was known for his heretical sorcery. The people came falsely to believe that "This man is the great power of God" (Acts 8:10). Later he tries to buy the power of the Holy Spirit from the apostles. "And when Simon saw that through laying on of the apostles' hands the Holy Ghost was given, he offered them money. Saying, Give me also this power, that on whomsoever I lay hands, he may receive the Holy Ghost. But Peter said unto him, Thy money perish with thee, because thou hast thought the gift of God may be purchased with money . . . thy heart is not right in the sight of God" (Acts 8:18–21). The name Simon is the root for *simony,* wrongful sale of religious blessing. In short, the name connotes venal corruption, an association Stowe clearly intends with her character Simon Legree.

Simon is also known as a Gnostic heretic who is distinguished by his prideful self-deification and contempt for the world. The Latin term for Simon was *Faustus,* and, as such, he became transmuted into the celebrated Faust figure whose overweening ambition and desire for absolute power lead him to make a pact with the devil. In the nineteenth century (particularly among the Romantics) the demonic overreacher/ outcast became a popular literary figure. Simon Legree belongs in this tradition of Faustian characters—figures like Cain and Captain Ahab— who are associated with evil and heresy. When Legree discovers Tom's piety, for example, he vows that he will destroy it, saying to him, "*I'm your church now!*" (482)—clearly the expression of demonic heresy.

Tom and eight other slaves Legree purchases (including Emmeline but not her mother, Susan) are transported to the Legree plantation, on the slave boat *Pirate.* The trip down the Red River occurs in a chapter entitled "The Middle Passage," the term used historically for the conveyance of blacks from Africa to America on slave ships. The Red River is another of the symbolic river passages in *Uncle Tom's Cabin* that help to structure the work. But it is also reminiscent of other literary waterways that signify a descent into an underworld, an infernal world of evil. In classical mythology Hades is bounded by riverways: in book VI of Virgil's *Aeneid* Aeneas must pass over the Acheron, which "boils with mud" (the Red River in *Uncle Tom's Cabin* was a "muddy, turbid current" [487]). The ferryman, Charon, like Legree, is "appallingly filthy . . . with a bush of unkempt/White beard . . . with eyes like jets of fire." (When Legree speaks to the slaves his eye is "glaring" [483].) Charon wears "a dirty cloak," and his craft is "rust-coloured."[2] Similarly, Dante's hell in the *Inferno* is bounded by various waterways. A more recent use of this topos may be seen in Joseph Conrad's 1902 novel, *Heart of Darkness,* which similarly involves a river passage into an evil terrain ruled over by the demonic Kurtz, a figure not unlike Simon Legree.

The Legree plantation is reached by an additional overland voyage on a "wild, forsaken road" that winds "through dreary pine barrens . . . long cyprus swamps, the doleful trees rising out of the slimy, spongy ground, hung with long wreaths of funeral black moss . . . [where a] mocassin snake might be sliding among broken stumps and sheltered branches that lay here and there, rotting in the water" (488). Clearly these images of decay and evil suggest a world beyond the pale of civilization. Indeed, the estate itself is in a fallen state of dissolution. The lawn is "covered with frowsy tangled grass . . . and the ground littered with broken pails, cobs of corn, and other slovenly remains. Here and there, a mildewed jessamine or honeysuckle hung raggedly. . . . What once was a large garden was now all grown over with weeds. What had been a conservatory had now no window-shades, and on the mouldering shelves stood some dry, forsaken flower-pots, with sticks in them, whose dried leaves showed they had once been plants" (491). The house itself is in a similar state of disrepair. Significantly, it is guarded by "three or four ferocious-looking dogs" (492). The gate to Hades in classical mythology was likewise watched over by a ferocious three-headed dog, Cerberus.

The torrid estate is the antithesis of the cool, orderly, clean, amiable models of domestic life we have encountered farther north. Legree's realm is ruled by the profit motive—"he used [the plantation], as he did everything else, merely as an implement for money making"

(491)—by hate (493), and by an arbitrary rule of force. Legree is an absolute capitalist tyrant, unchecked by the restraining cultural feminist ethic of white women—there are none on the plantation—or by rule of law. He has, in effect, turned the plantation into a slave labor camp where slaves are routinely worked to death. Here Stowe turns on its head the myth perpetrated in the plantation novels that the southern plantation presented a benign pastoral alternative to the harsh industrial North. Instead what we have is a kind of rural factory where workers' lives are brutalized through relentless, alienated labor.[3] In the economy of the Legree plantation production is for exchange, rather than for use, as in the domestic economies further north, and the workers are themselves the prime commodities.

The slaves are kept in a degraded and debased condition. One of the first actions Legree takes toward Tom is to divest him of his personal belongings—always a means of demoralizing a person. Through the relentless labor, the filth they must live in, the meager rations (their dinner consists of one piece of cornbread [494]), the lack of love and religion, and perhaps most of all the absence of hope, the slaves become wholly dehumanized, even behaving toward one another with callous, self-protective indifference. "Every one of them would turn against you, the first time they got a chance. They are all of 'em as low and cruel to each other as they can be" (513).

The overseers on the plantation are collaborative blacks, Sambo and Quimbo. "Legree had trained them in savageness and brutality" (492). Stowe shows insight into the master-slave relationship in observing that "It is a common remark, and one that is supposed to militate strongly against the character of the race, that the negro overseer is always more tyrannical and cruel that the white one. This is simply saying that the negro mind has been more crushed and debased than the white. It is no more true of this race than of every oppressed race, the world over. The slave is always a tyrant, if he can get a chance to be one" (492–93). Thus, the cycle of violence, of domination-dominated, perpetuates itself unless broken by a refusal to play the power game of objectifying one's "other" and denying his or her humanity—the philosophy of Christian nonviolent resistance practiced by Uncle Tom.

Here the use of black women sexually is more explicit than else-where. Emmeline has been purchased by Simon to serve as his mistress, and a mulatto woman, Lucy, purchased for Sambo. Lucy protests that she has left a husband back in New Orleans, which Legree, of course, ignores. Ironically, Sambo treats Lucy more as a wife than a mistress, which allows Stowe to bring out briefly the feminist leitmotiv of husbands' enslavement of wives. He says, "Wal, Lucy, yo my woman now. Yo grind dis yer corn, and get *my* supper baked, ye har?" She responds, "I an't your woman, and I won't be," whereupon he replies with a threat of violence, "I'll kick you, then!" (495). Legree also indulges in fits of violence, largely induced by heavy drinking, which enables Stowe to introduce the temperance theme, one of her social causes.

Within this degradation, however, are "anticipatory illuminations" of another realm. These instances of a negative dialectic are provided through music and through dreams. While Legree refuses to permit Tom to sing hymns, allowing the slaves to sing only "unmeaning" ditties, the soulful way they intone the melody expresses their utopian longings. "[N]o wail of despair, no words of impassioned prayer, could have had such a depth of woe in them as the wild notes of the chorus. As if the poor, dumb heart, threatened,—prisoned,—took refuge in that inarticulate sanctuary of music, and found there a language in which to breathe its prayer to God!" (490). Later, after moments of dark despair, Tom has a dream of Eva in heaven that reanimates his hope and faith (498–99).

Since the slaves are stupefied by the brutality they daily endure, they are mystified at first by Tom's simple gestures of Christian charity and talk about God. But a new field hand, a woman, warns Tom that helping the other slaves with their work will get him in trouble (he has been helping Lucy fill her cotton basket because she was falling behind her quota). "You know nothing about this place," she warned, "or you wouldn't have done that. When you've been here a month, you'll be done helping anybody; you'll find it hard enough to take care of your own skin!" Tom protests, "The Lord forbid, Missis!" But she replies bitterly, "The Lord never visits these parts" (504). Tom indeed does get into trouble when the overseers realize he has been padding Lucy's load. Sambo is already seeking revenge on Lucy for rejecting him, but Legree cannot afford to lose a laborer in the height of the season, so he rejects the idea of flogging her. As a compromise he orders Tom to flog her, thinking Tom will give her only a mild beating and thus not seriously injure his property. Legree has also been annoyed and unnerved by Tom's "tenderness of feeling" (500), which he finds vaguely subversive on a place governed by "*hardness*" and therefore requiring eradication (501).

Tom, however, refuses to beat Lucy—thus initiating a sustained confrontation between him and Legree. First, Legree strikes Tom across the face with a whip. But Tom insists that he cannot beat the woman: "This yer thing I can't feel it right to do;—and, Mas'r, I *never* shall do it,—*never!*" (507). Tom's defiance enrages Legree, but Tom persists, saying, "if you mean to kill me, kill me; but, as to my raising my hand agin any one here, I never shall,—I'll die first" (508). Legree becomes violent, asserting his authority and kicking Tom: "An't I yer master? . . . An't yer mine, now, body and soul?" (508). But once again Tom responds with quiet and courageous defiance, "No! no! no! my soul an't yours, Mas'r!" (508). It is this kind of refusal to capitulate before brutal treatment that belies the unfortunate popular stereotype of Uncle Tom as a craven collaborator and elevates him to the status of a modern existentialist hero, comparable, as Moody Prior has pointed out, to the defiant characters of contemporary Russian author Aleksandr Solzhenitsyn, who confront their torturers in Soviet gulags.[4] Tom's stand, however, only infuriates Legree, who turns him over to his torturers, Sambo and Quimbo, who are, Stowe says, a "personification of the powers of darkness"; they then beat him "unresisting" nearly to death (509).

The mysterious new field hand who had warned Tom to be careful is Cassy, one of Stowe's most fascinating and complex characters, daringly introduced late in the novel. Cassy is a kind of Mary Magdalene; for five years she has been forced to serve as Legree's concubine. Earlier kept for a period as mistress of a white man she grew to love, Cassy was nevertheless sold by him along with her two children—

Henry and Elise—to pay off a debt. Her new owner also used her sexually, threatening to sell her children if she resisted. Despite her attempts to keep him mollified, he sold the children behind her back. Later when she discovered her son being beaten—a gruesome scene— she tried to kill her master, and he sold her to another owner. After bearing another child, she found she could not endure the thought of its growing up in slavery, and she killed it. After several more masters she finally ends up with Legree.

Cassy's experience has left her bitter, defiant, and an atheist. "[H]er face was deeply wrinkled with lines of pain, and of proud and bitter endurance. . . . [H]er whole form [was] emaciated . . . [and] in her eye was a deep, settled night of anguish" (501). In the field, "she picked very fast and very clean, and with an air of scorn, as if she despised both the work and the disgrace and humiliation" (502). When harassed by one of the drivers, she retorts defiantly, making him back off. "[W]ith quivering lip and dilated nostrils, she drew herself up, and fixed a glance, blazing with rage and scorn, on the driver. . . . '[T]ouch *me*, if you dare!'" (504). She even has a power over Legree because he thinks she is possessed. When he makes an advance, she responds with "a glance so wild and insane . . . as to be almost appalling. 'You're afraid of me Simon. . . . I've got the devil in me'" (525).

Because of this she is able to blunt his venom against Tom. In a scene that is an ironic counterpoint to Mrs. Shelby's petition of her husband, Cassy uses an economic argument to convince Legree to lay off Tom momentarily at least. She reminds him that to put Tom, an able-bodied worker, out of commission at the height of the cotton-picking season would mean a slackening of production. Legree has a bet with local planters that he will produce the largest harvest. Although he rejects her "meddling in business," as Mr. Shelby did his wife, he follows her advice (537, 540).

While Cassy is an alcoholic and an atheist—she cannot pray; she can only "hate and curse" (562)—she is the only one compassionate enough to minister to Tom after his brutal beating, bringing him water and bathing his wounds. Once again she warns Tom that resistance is futile; he is "in the devil's hands" (511). "There's no law here, of God or man" (512). As time passes, she and Tom get into theological debates about God's existence and Tom's philosophy of nonresistance, which gradually begins to affect her. "[E]ven the half-crazed and wandering mind of Cassy was soothed and calmed by his simple and unobtrusive influences" (560). Nevertheless, one evening, "stung to madness and despair by the crushing agonies of a life," Cassy resolves to kill Legree and enlists Tom's aid. She has drugged Legree's brandy and provided an axe for Tom to do the deed (she fears she is not physically strong enough to pull it off). But Tom refuses, saying "good never comes of wickedness" and that we must "love our enemies" (561). He suggests that she and Emmeline try to escape instead. But when Cassy asks Tom to come too, he refuses in terms similar to those he offered at the Shelby plantation, saying he has the moral strength to endure persecution while she does not. He also has come to feel he has a mission to spread the gospel among the heathen slaves at the plantation. "I'll stay with 'em and bear my cross with 'em till the end" (562). In the end, Tom dies protecting Cassy and Emmeline, refusing under intense torture to reveal their whereabouts and thus enabling their escape.

Because of his profane and "godless" state, Legree is given to superstition about the supernatural world. The specters he conjures up seem to be projections of his own conscience. "No one," Stowe says, "is so thoroughly superstitious as the godless man. . . . Life and death to him are haunted grounds, filled with goblin forms of vague and shadowy dread" (567). The first indication of Legree's weakness in this regard occurs when Sambo brings him Tom's tokens—the silver dollar George had given him and the lock of Eva's hair—which he had discovered during the beating. Sambo tells him that "it's a witch thing. . . . Something that niggers gets from witches. Keeps 'em from feelin' when they's flogged" (527). Legree is horrified by the talismen. Under the influence of "a dread, unhallowed necromancy of evil," he burns the hair—along with a letter his dying mother had written him; "when he saw them hissing and crackling in the flame, inwardly he shuddered as he thought of everlasting fires" (529). (Recall that Simon Magus in the New Testament was an evil necromancer or sorcerer.)

The lock of Eva's hair has reminded Legree of his New England mother, a long-suffering and devoted woman who had pleaded with him to reform and remains in his memory as a kind of tormenting conscience. For "one night, when his mother, in the last agony of her despair, knelt at his feet, he spurned her from him,—threw her senseless on the floor, and, with brutal curses, fled to his ship" (528–29). After her death, a lock of her hair had been sent to him, along with word that she had forgiven him. After burning Eva's hair, Legree hears Emmeline singing a hymn about the last judgment, which further spooks him. He comes to believe that Tom's relics were indeed charmed and that somehow Tom had secured the lock of his mother's hair. "I b'lieve I am bewitched, sure enough!" he exclaims, vowing to leave Tom alone in the future (531). After much drinking, Legree has a feverish dream about his mother in which "she turned away from him, and he fell down, down, down, amid a confused noise of shrieks, and groans, and shouts of demon laughter" (536).

Cassy bases her escape plan on her knowledge of Legree's fear of the demonic supernatural. She begins planting suggestions that the garret of the house is haunted. She complains that she cannot sleep at night because of all the groans and scuffling she hears coming from the attic (566); she reads Legree ghost stories (568–69); and she fixes an empty bottle in the attic in such a way that it emits sounds like a shriek in heavy winds (566). Having thoroughly terrified Legree about the attic, she unobtrusively moves her and Emmeline's belongings up there. Then she and Emmeline make their escape through the swamp bordering the estate and then circling back to the rear entrance of the house, which is deserted, since all are out chasing the fugitives. They hole up in the attic, knowing that Legree will never come up there. From this hideout they plan to make a final escape later, dressed as ghosts (in white sheets). This they do—Legree, once again in a drunken state, thinks the sheet is "his mother's shroud" (596). Once off the plantation they dress in Creole outfits, with Cassy acting as a lady traveling north and Emmeline as her servant. (Cassy has also stolen some money to finance their trip.)

Meanwhile, in the garret the two women's relationship intensifies. At first, Cassy tries to keep the girl at a distance emotionally. When Emmeline takes her hand in a comforting way, Cassy cries, "Don't! . . . you'll get me to loving you; and I never mean to love anything again" (580). But Emmeline says perhaps when they are free Cassy will be able to relocate her daughter (as it turns out Eliza is Cassy's long-lost daughter, and the two are reunited). In the meantime, she says she will be "like a daughter" to Cassy. "I shall love you, Cassy, whether you love me or not!" (580). Cassy is softened by this pledge and puts her arm around Emmeline. She says if "God would give me back my children, then I could pray." Emmeline says they must have hope (580).

Feminist critics Sandra Gilbert and Susan Gubar have an interesting interpretation of Cassy, seeing her as an archetypal example of "the madwoman in the attic," the title of their work on (primarily) nineteenth-century women's literature. In *Uncle Tom's Cabin,* they claim, Stowe presents "a uniquely female model of liberation" in Cassy's escape scheme. "[A] madwoman herself, she plans to liberate herself and the girl Emmeline . . . by exploiting the story of the madwoman in the attic." Dressed as a ghost, "she *is* in a sense the ghost of her dead self, the self Legree killed by his abuse." "[T]his veiled woman represents [Legree's] denial of his mother, of mother love, and mother right. Guilty of matricide . . . Legree never can forget that deadly angel."[5] In other words, Cassy's story expresses a kind of demonic female revenge.

One cannot, however, ignore the role of Tom in their escape. In a rage over the successful disappearance of the two women but suspecting that they are still in the vicinity, Legree turns on Tom, hoping to torture out of him information about their whereabouts (578; 581). Tom had also refused to join in their chase, which further infuriated Legree.

After the first beating Tom had experienced a period of deep depression in which his faith—not to mention his life—nearly flickered out. Sent back to grueling field labor long before his wounds had healed, Tom returned every evening to his cabin so exhausted that he could no longer read his Bible; nor had he time to communicate much with the other slaves. In this state of utter isolation his "religious peace and trust" gave way "to tossings of soul and despondent darkness. The gloomiest problem of this mysterious life was constantly before his eyes—souls crushed and ruined, evil triumphant, and God silent" (552).

At this moment Legree comes to tempt and taunt him, saying that if he had been cooperative he would have had a special status on the plantation. "You might have been better off than Sambo, or Quimbo . . . ye might have had liberty to lord it round, and cut up the other niggers; and ye might have had, now and then, a good warming of whiskey punch." Legree urges him to throw his Bible in the fire and collaborate with his master. "Come, Tom, don't you think you'd better be reasonable?—heave that ar old pack of trash in the fire, and join my church!" (553). Simon Legree here comes to represent the devil or the Antichrist, whose "church" is one of evil and darkness.

Legree's contemptuous behavior has the ironic effect of reawakening Tom's faith so that a kind of dialectical inversion occurs. "The atheistic taunts of his cruel master sunk his before dejected soul to the lowest ebb"; he hangs on to his faith with only "a numb, despairing grasp." In this moment, however, a vision appears to him: "of one crowned with thorns, buffeted and bleeding." Experiencing "floods of emotion" Tom sees the vision change: "the sharp thorns became rays of glory" (554). Here Tom is undergoing the emotionally intense conversion experience that constitutes a "visible sign" of election in the theology of Edwardsean Calvinism. Reinspired by his vision, in which Christ promises Tom personal redemption, Tom finds his faith buoyed and his resistance to Legree intensified. Stowe earlier designated Tom a martyr (541), which is the title of the chapter that covers his death, but Tom is really more than a martyr; he becomes more nearly a Christ.

When Tom appears impervious to a lashing by Legree for singing hymns, the biblical words echo in Legree's mind, haunting him: "What have we to do with thee, thou Jesus of Nazareth?—art thou come to torment us before the time" (558). Tom meanwhile continues his compassionate acts of charity with the field hands, which are beginning "to awaken long-silent chords in their benumbed hearts." He begins at last "to have a strange power over them" (559).

The final, agonizing scene where Tom is beaten to death is conceived in terms of the Crucifixion. When Quimbo comes to fetch Tom in the field for the final beating, Tom sets down his basket and says, "Into thy hands I commend my spirit!" (581)—Jesus' last words on the cross. Earlier, during his dark period of despair Tom had cried out, "O Jesus! Lord Jesus! have you quite forgot us poor critturs" (513), recalling Christ's "My God, my God, why hast thou forsaken me?" Tom's final torture has, however, a modern cast, in that Tom dies at the hands of an executioner who is trying to coerce information from him (about Cassy and Emmeline's location). Legree says, "I've made up my mind to KILL YOU . . . unless you'll tell me what you know about these yer gals!" Tom replies, "*I han't got nothing to tell, Mas'r.*" Legree then asks him if it is because he does not know where the women are, but Tom acknowledges that he knows but will not tell (582). Legree becomes obsessed with destroying Tom—almost as Ahab does the white whale in Melville's *Moby-Dick*—while Tom remains heroically compassionate toward Legree to the end, saying "I'd *give* ye my heart's blood" (582).

Tom is briefly tempted in his dying moments to betray the women, but he resists. His last words are ones of forgiveness to his persecutors, similar to Christ's "forgive them, for they know not what they do" (Luke 24:34). Like one of the thieves crucified with Jesus, Sambo and Quimbo experience a religious awakening as Tom dies. Thus, Tom endures physical death but has the final spiritual victory in his mighty confrontation with the powers of darkness, symbolized in Simon Legree.

11

Conclusion

The remainder of the novel (chapters 41–45) brings to more or less happy conclusion the fates of the other black characters. These final episodes form a kind of resurrectory coda, following and in a way proceeding from the sacrificial death of Tom.

Two days after Tom's fatal flogging but before Tom has finally expired, Master George Shelby, who has been searching for Tom for some time, reaches the Legree plantation—too late to revive Tom, who is near death. Tom is conscious enough, however, to realize that George has come to buy him back, thus fulfilling the promise he and his mother made years before. Tom asks George to spare Chloe the details of his suffering and death and dies with a heart full of Christian love. His final words are " 'Pears like I loves 'em all! I loves every creatur', everywhar!—it's nothing *but* love! O, Mas'r George! What a thing 't is to be a Christian! . . . Who,—who,—shall separate us from the love of Christ?" (591).

George then carefully prepares the body for burial, while Legree sarcastically comments, "What a fuss, for a dead nigger!" (592). The remark incenses George, who smashes Legree in the face with his fist, knocking him flat on the ground. George wraps Tom's body in a cloak, and he and two of the slaves bury him in an unmarked grave near the plantation. The blacks ask George to buy them, but he says he cannot, vowing nevertheless to free his own slaves.

Meanwhile, Cassy and Emmeline, disguised as Creoles, book passage north on the same Mississippi riverboat as George Shelby. In another somewhat contrived coincidence a Madame de Thoux also happens to be on the boat. As it turns out, she is George Harris's missing sister, whose fate has been happier than predicted. Her master had set her free and married her, and she had recently inherited his estate. In telling the woman about her brother George, young Shelby mentions that he had married a beautiful young slave of theirs, whom Mr. Shelby had bought in New Orleans from a man named Simmons. On hearing this, Cassy, who has been listening to the conversation, faints: she realizes that Eliza is her daughter.

Shortly thereafter Cassy, Emmeline, and Emily de Thoux (George's sister) make their way to Canada where they reunite with the Harrises, who have by now lived in freedom for five years. (As noted, Stowe was casual about the time spans covered in the novel; indeed, there appears to be a discrepancy between the two periods that are specifically given, the five-year span from Tom's sale until his death [615] and the five-year period of the Harrises' stay in Canada [603]. The Harrises, in fact, arrive in Canada shortly before Tom's death, and Cassy and company make their way to Canada in a much shorter time than five years.)

In any event, the reunion among the various family members is a happy one. Cassy becomes a Christian, and Emily gives George money for the education he has always desired, which he elects to pursue in France. Cassy's son also turns up and Emmeline marries. We also learn that Topsy becomes a missionary in Africa. A few figures seem to have been forgotten; we never learn what happens to Emmeline's mother, Susan, or to the slave Lucy, or to Mammy and Adolph, as well as scores of others we have met in passing along the way. Perhaps Stowe leaves their fate obscure deliberately, befitting the reality of millions of slaves.

George Harris, as noted earlier, conceives the idea of a Christian African republic, a Liberia, where American slaves can return home

(608–12). This idea was roundly criticized and rejected by blacks after the novel was published, and Stowe came to regret its formulation. Nevertheless, it expresses a kind of utopian projection of a peaceable kingdom, a socialist republic that operates according to Christian principles—in other words, Stowe's own ideal of a model society.

Meanwhile, George Shelby breaks the news of Tom's death to his mother and to Aunt Chloe back in Kentucky. George's action of freeing his slaves, paying them wages, and providing them with educations— the voluntary emancipation Ophelia urged on St. Clare—is another solution Stowe presents to the slavery problem. George says that he made his resolution over Tom's grave and says that "UNCLE TOM'S CABIN" should serve as a memorial to Tom and to his sacrificial death (617).

The last chapter, which Stowe prepared for the book publication of the novel, is a kind of exhortatory peroration in which she summarizes the arguments she has presented against slavery. Once again she claims that much of her material was based on real incident; that slavery as a system is evil and must be abolished; and that while she tried to depict it in "a *living dramatic reality*" (623), she realizes that "nothing of tragedy can be written . . . that equals the frightful reality of scenes daily and hourly acting on our shores" (623).

As for remedies, she counsels principally the change of heart we have noted she saw as necessary for any true social reform to occur. "There is one thing that every individual can do,—they can see to it that *they feel right*" (624). By expressing their aversion to slavery, people can gradually extend their influence, thus changing the climate of public opinion on the subject. Stowe also advocates prayer, education of freed slaves, and a kind of affirmative action for them (625) before they are returned to Africa (626). Finally, she predicts God's vengeance will fall if the nation does not act to end the injustice of slavery (629). On this prophetic note, Stowe concludes her mighty novel.

Years later, at Stowe's death in 1896, her closest friend, Annie Adams Fields, fittingly summed up Stowe's life and work. "A great spirit," she wrote simply, "has performed its mission."

Notes and References

Chapter 1

1. Charles H. Foster, *The Rungless Ladder* (1954; reprint ed., New York: Cooper Square, 1970), 231.

2. Ibid., 55.

3. For a useful survey see John Hope Franklin, *From Slavery to Freedom: A History of Negro Americans*, 3d ed. (New York: Knopf, 1967), esp. chaps. 4, 6, 10–13.

4. As cited in Moira Davison Reynolds, *"Uncle Tom's Cabin" and Mid-Nineteenth Century United States* (Jefferson, N.C.: McFarland, 1985), 117.

5. For details about the "real" sources for *Uncle Tom's Cabin*, see *The Key to "Uncle Tom's Cabin"* (1853; reprint ed., New York: Arno and the New York Times, 1968), and *Life and Letters of Harriet Beecher Stowe*, ed. Annie Adams Fields (Boston: Houghton, Mifflin, 1898), 175–76.

6. On cultural feminism see Josephine Donovan, *Feminist Theory: The Intellectual Traditions of American Feminism* (New York: Ungar, 1985), chap. 2; on Stowe's feminism see Josephine Donovan, "Harriet Beecher Stowe's Feminism," *American Transcendental Quarterly* 47–48 (Summer–Fall 1980):141–57; also essential is Jean Fagan Yellin, "Doing It Herself: *Uncle Tom's Cabin* and Women's Role in the Slavery Crisis," in *New Essays on "Uncle Tom's Cabin,"* ed. Eric J. Sundquist (Cambridge: Cambridge University Press, 1986), 85–105, and Gillian Brown, "Getting in the Kitchen with Dinah: Domestic Politics in *Uncle Tom's Cabin*," *American Quarterly* 36, no. 4 (Fall 1984):513–16.

7. Fields, *Life and Letters*, 110; Edmund Wilson, *Patriotic Gore* (New York: Oxford University Press, 1962), 30; Forrest Wilson, *Crusader in Crinoline* (Philadelphia: Lippincott, 1941), 204 (Dutton Letter); Leslie A. Fiedler, *The Inadvertent Epic* (New York: Simon & Schuster, 1979), 33; the Brontë quote is in Ellen Moers, *Literary Women* (Garden City, N.Y.: Anchor Doubleday, 1977), 27; John R. Adams, *Harriet Beecher Stowe* (New York: Twayne, 1963), 27. See also Constance Rourke, *Trumpets of Jubilee* (New York: Har-

court, Brace, 1927), 107–08. Rourke suggests that Calvinism was another tyranny against which Stowe rebelled in *Uncle Tom's Cabin.*

8. Fields, *Life and Letters,* 173. See also Stowe's wrenching account of her son's death (119).

9. Foster, *Rungless Ladder,* x–xi, 98, 22, 134; Alice Crozier, *The Novels of Harriet Beecher Stowe* (New York: Oxford University Press, 1969), 19–21.

10. Sydney E. Ahlstrom, *A Religious History of the American People* (New Haven: Yale University Press, 1972), 303. See chap. 19 for a useful survey of Edwards's thought. Also see Amy Schrager Lang, *Prophetic Women* (Berkeley: University of California Press, 1987), 78–81, 102–05. Stowe did not accept all of Edwards's ideas uncritically. In 1840 she refuted his doctrine on the will in an article, "Free Agency" (Wilson, *Patriotic Gore,* 38). After *Uncle Tom's Cabin* Stowe moved steadily away from Calvinism. See especially her novel *The Minister's Wooing* (1859).

11. Ibid., 80.

12. Ibid., 427.

13. *Key to "Uncle Tom's Cabin,"* 28, 42; E. Bruce Kirkham, *The Building of "Uncle Tom's Cabin"* (Knoxville: University of Tennessee Press, 1977), 83, 85, 92, 100–02; Sundquist, Introduction to *New Essays,* 17.

14. On the former, see Jean Fagan Yellin, *The Intricate Knot* (New York: New York University Press, 1972), 85–98; on the latter, see William R. Taylor, *Cavalier and Yankee* (New York: Braziller, 1961), esp. 308–13.

15. Philip Fisher, *Hard Facts* (New York: Oxford University Press, 1985), 87–127.

16. There is no evidence Stowe read *Dead Souls;* however, Wilson, *Patriotic Gore,* 10, also notes the similarity between the two works.

17. In places it exhibits aspects of the Menippean satire, a particular form of realism in which representative character types are anatomized into their constituent traits. See Northrup Frye, *Anatomy of Criticism* (Princeton: Princeton University Press, 1957), 309–12. In *Uncle Tom's Cabin* some of these types take on allegorical significance; indeed in the latter sections the work often borders on allegory. On this point and for an effective interpretation of *Uncle Tom's Cabin* as a sentimentalist novel see Jane Tompkins, "Sentimental Power: *Uncle Tom's Cabin* and the Politics of Literary History," in *The New Feminist Criticism,* ed. Elaine Showalter (New York: Pantheon, 1985), 81–104. On *Uncle Tom's Cabin* as a realist novel see especially Kenneth Lynn, Introduction to *Uncle Tom's Cabin* (Cambridge: Harvard University Press, 1962), viii–xxiii. Fred Gared See considers Stowe's use of metonymy in *Uncle Tom's Cabin;* see his "Metaphoric and Metonymic Imagery in Nineteenth Century American Fiction: Harriet Beecher Stowe, Rebecca Harding Davis,

and Harold Frederick," (Ph.D. diss., University of California, Berkeley, 1967), 96–106.

18. For a survey of Stowe's other works, seen in the tradition of "women's realism," see Josephine Donovan, *New England Local Color Literature: A Women's Tradition* (New York: Ungar, 1983), chap. 4.

19. Erich Auerbach, *Mimesis: The Representation of Reality in Western Literature* (1953; reprint ed., New York: Anchor, 1957), 216–19. Cotton Mather's *Magnalia* (1702), which Stowe acknowledged as having strongly influenced her, similarly connects earthly events to God's design but also manifests an inherent interest in those events in and of themselves. See the *Magnalia Christi Americana; or, the Ecclesiastical History of New England*, ed. and abr. Raymond J. Cunningham (1702; reprint ed. New York: Ungar, 1970), esp. chap. 6, "A Book of Memorable Events." As other New England Puritans, Mather believed New Englanders to have a special covenant with God, an idea Stowe seems to have accepted.

Chapter 2

1. *Great Soviet Encyclopedia*, 3d ed., vol. 3 (New York: Macmillan, 1980), 765; Margaret Holbrook Hildreth, *Harriet Beecher Stowe: A Bibliography* (Hamden, Conn.: Archon, 1976).

2. Van Wyck Brooks, *Literature in New England: The Flowering of New England, 1815–1865* (Garden City, N.Y.: Garden City Publishing Co., 1944), 421.

3. Sundquist, Introduction to *New Essays*, 3.

4. Moody E. Prior, "Mrs. Stowe's Uncle Tom," *Critical Inquiry* 5 (Summer 1979):650.

5. *The Minister's Wooing* (1859; reprint ed. Ridgewood, N.J.: Gregg Press, 1968), 50. See also Foster, *Rungless Ladder*, 122.

6. Victor E. Frankl, *Man's Search for Meaning* (New York: Washington Square Press, 1963), 31, 99–100, 105–06.

7. Martin Buber, *I and Thou*, trans. Walter Kaufmann (New York: Scribner's, 1970).

8. See especially Iris Murdoch, *The Sovereignty of Good* (New York: Scribner's, 1971), 34, 37, 66. The concept of "attentive love" is from Simone Weil, *Waiting for God* (1950), in *The Simone Weil Reader*, ed. George A. Punichas (New York: David McKay, 1977), 44–52. Note also that contemporary feminist theorist Sara Ruddick sees the concept as crucial to a maternal ethic in *Maternal Thinking: Toward a Politics of Peace* (Boston: Beacon Press, 1989), 119–23. Stowe seems to have anticipated Ruddick's thesis.

9. See especially Rita Nakashima Brock, *Journeys by Heart: A Christology of Erotic Power* (New York: Crossroad, 1988).

10. Martin Luther King, Jr., *Stride Toward Freedom* (1958), as excerpted in *Nonviolence in America: A Documentary History,* ed. Staughton Lynd (Indianapolis: Bobbs-Merrill, 1966), 388.

11. Ellen Moers, "Mrs. Stowe's Vengeance," *New York Review of Books,* 3 September 1970, 30.

Chapter 3

1. Letter of Charles Kingsley to Stowe, 12 August 1852, in Stowe's 1896 introduction to *Uncle Tom's Cabin, The Writings of Harriet Beecher Stowe,* vol. 1 (1896; reprint ed., New York: AMS Press, 1967), lxxi–ii.

2. Leo Tolstoy, *What Is Art?,* trans. Almyer Maude (Indianapolis: Bobbs-Merrill, 1960), 152.

3. Thomas F. Gossett, *"Uncle Tom's Cabin" and American Culture* (Dallas: Southern Methodist University Press, 1985), 340–41.

4. For excerpts from southern views see Arthur Bartlett Maurice, "Famous Novels and Their Contemporary Critics," *Bookman* 17 (March 1903): 23–30; see also Gossett, *"Uncle Tom's Cabin,"* 185.

5. *The Life and Writings of Frederick Douglass,* ed. Philip S. Foner, vol. 2, *Pre–Civil War Decade, 1850–1860* (New York: International Publishers, 1950), 227–28.

6. As recorded in *Slave Testimonies: Two Centuries of Letters, Speeches, Interviews, and Autobiographies,* ed. John W. Blassingame (Baton Rouge: Louisiana State University Press, 1977), 723.

7. Gossett, *"Uncle Tom's Cabin,"* 362.

8. Ibid., 361.

9. *Liberator* 22, no. 13 (26 March 1852):50.

10. Henry C. Wright, letter to *Liberator* 22, no. 28 (9 July 1852):11; "Reply to Henry C. Wright, On 'Uncle Tom's Cabin,' " *Liberator* 22, no. 38 (17 September 1852): 152. Other useful summaries of the black response to *Uncle Tom's Cabin* are in Gossett, *"Uncle Tom's Cabin,"* 172–74, and Yellin, *Intricate Knot,* 138–39.

11. Martin Delany, "Uncle Tom" (1853), as cited in Richard Yarborough, "Strategies of Black Characterization in *Uncle Tom's Cabin* and the Early Afro-American Novel," in *New Essays,* 71; see also 68–70.

12. Gossett, *"Uncle Tom's Cabin,"* 294.

13. Yarborough, "Strategies," 68; Mary Church Terrell, *Harriet Beecher Stowe: An Appreciation* (Washington, D.C.: Murray Brothers, 1911); James Weldon Johnson, *The Autobiography of an Ex-Coloured Man* (1912; reprint

Notes and References

ed., New York: Knopf, 1951), 41–42; Langston Hughes, Preface to *Uncle Tom's Cabin* (New York: Dodd, Mead, 1952); W. E. B. DuBois, "Books," *Crisis* (March 1931), in *Writings* (New York: Library of America, 1986), 1234; see also Gossett, "*Uncle Tom's Cabin*," 363.

14. James Baldwin, "Everybody's Protest Novel," *Notes of a Native Son* (Boston: Beacon Press, 1955), 13–23; Alex Haley, "In 'Uncle Tom' Are Our Guilt and Our Hope," *New York Times Magazine*, 1 March 1964, 23, 90.

15. See espcially Monrose Gwin, *Black and White Women of the Old South* (Knoxville: University of Tennessee Press, 1985), 20–32; Hortense J. Spillers, "Changing the Letter: The Yokes, the Jokes of Discourse, or, Mrs. Stowe, Mr. Reed," in *Slavery and the Literary Imagination*, Selected Papers from the English Institute, 1987, n.s., no. 13 (Baltimore: Johns Hopkins University Press, 1989), 25–61; Yarborough, "Strategies," 45–84; and Yellin, *Intricate Knot*, 147.

16. George M. Frederickson, *The Black Image in the White Mind* (New York: Harper, 1971), 13 n. 22, 101–14.

17. For summaries see Jean Ashton, *Harriet Beecher Stowe: A Reference Guide* (Boston: G. K. Hall, 1977). The only exceptions to this general dismissal were Rourke, *Trumpets of Jubilee* (1927), and Brooks, *Flowering of New England* (1936).

18. Leslie A. Fiedler, *Love and Death in the American Novel* (New York: Criterion Books, 1960), 261; Wilson, *Patriotic Gore*, 5–7; Henry James, *A Small Boy and Others* (New York: Scribner's, 1913); Edward Wagenknecht, *Harriet Beecher Stowe* (New York: Oxford University Press, 1965), 164. Tompkins, "Sentimental Power," 101 n. 8, also notes this condescension.

19. Lynn, Introduction to *Uncle Tom's Cabin*, xi–xii; Anthony Burgess, "Making de White Boss Frown," *Encounter* 27, no. 1 (July 1966): 55–56.

20. Frederick Crews, "Whose American Renaissance?," *New York Review of Books*, 27 October 1988, 75 n. 7.

21. Nina Baym, "Melodramas of Beset Manhood: How Theories of American Fiction Exclude Women Authors," *American Quarterly* 33 (Summer 1981): 123–39; Sundquist, Introduction to *New Essays*, 2.

22. Tompkins, "Sentimental Power," 84–85.

23. Fisher, *Hard Facts*, 116, 118.

24. David S. Reynolds, *Beneath the American Renaissance* (New York: Knopf, 1988), 77; Ann Douglas, *The Feminization of American Culture* (1977; reprint ed., New York: Avon, 1978), 2, 12–13; Lawrence Buell, *New England Literary Culture* (Cambridge: Cambridge University Press, 1986), 188.

25. Helen Waite Papashvily, *All the Happy Endings* (New York: Harper, 1956); Moers, *Literary Women*, 27.

26. Elizabeth Ammons, "Heroines in *Uncle Tom's Cabin*," *American Literature* 49, no. 2 (May 1977): 163, 171, 178; Yellin, "Doing It Herself," 91, 101–02.

27. Elaine Showalter, "Piecing and Writing," in *The Poetics of Gender*, ed. Nancy K. Miller (New York: Columbia University Press, 1986), 222–47.

28. Spillers, "Changing the Letter," 36, 45.

29. Brown, "Getting in the Kitchen," 507–08, 511.

30. *Marxism and Art: Essays Classic and Contemporary*, ed. Maynard Solomon (1973; reprint ed., Detroit: Wayne State University Press, 1979), 241.

31. Mikhail Bakhtin, *Problems of Dostoievsky's Poetics* (1929), trans. R. W. Rotsel (n.p.: Ardis, 1973), 14, 51, 70.

32. Jack Zipes, Introduction to *The Utopian Function of Art and Literature*, by Ernst Bloch (Cambridge, Mass.: MIT Press, 1988), xxvi–vii; Fredric Jameson, *The Political Unconscious: Narrative as a Socially Symbolic Act* (Ithaca: Cornell University Press, 1981), 79; Solomon, *Marxism and Art*, 468. For a further elaboration of these ideas see Josephine Donovan, "Radical Feminist Criticism," Introduction to *Feminist Literary Criticism: Explorations in Theory*, 2d ed. (Lexington: University Press of Kentucky, 1989).

Chapter 4

1. Charles Edward Stowe, *Life of Harriet Beecher Stowe* (Boston: Houghton, Mifflin, 1889), 153.

2. As edited in Kirkham, *Building*, 16.

3. Stowe articulates her theory of style in "Faults of Inexperienced Writers," *Hearth and Home* 1, no. 5 (23 January 1869):72; Moers, *Literary Women*, 96–97.

4. On Stowe's use of this convention see Robyn R. Warhol, "Toward a Theory of the Engaging Narrator: Earnest Intervention in Gaskell, Stowe, and Eliot," *PMLA* 101, no. 5 (October 1986): 811–18.

5. Kirkham, *Building*, 67; *Key to "Uncle Tom's Cabin*," 1.

6. Rachel Blau DuPlessis, "For the Etruscans," *New Feminist Criticism*, 278.

7. Fisher, *Hard Facts*, 116–17.

8. A similar argument with respect to animals is used against animal rights advocates today. See Josephine Donovan, "Animal Rights and Feminist Theory." *Signs* 15, no. 2 (Winter 1990):350–75, and Marjorie Spiegel, *The Dreaded Comparison: Race and Animal Slavery* (Philadelphia: New Society Publishers, 1988). Interestingly, Stowe was not insensitive to the animal rights issue; she wrote a treatise, "Rights of Dumb Animals," *Hearth and Home* 1,

no. 2 (2 January 1869):24, and makes numerous comparisons in *Uncle Tom's Cabin* between the treatment of slaves and animals.

9. Frantz Fanon, *Black Skin, White Masks* (New York: Grove Press, 1967); see also discussion in Donovan, *Feminist Theory,* 137–39.

Chapter 5

1. Karl Marx, *Critique of Political Economy* (1859), *Karl Marx: Selected Writings,* ed. David McLellan (Oxford: Oxford University Press, 1977), 389.

2. *Minister's Wooing,* 15. A number of contemporary feminists have argued similarly that women exhibit a less abstract form of moral reasoning than men. See especially Carol Gilligan, *In a Different Voice: Psychological Theory and Women's Development* (Cambridge: Harvard University Press, 1982). Donovan, *Feminist Theory,* 173–78, summarizes these theories. On men's repression of the personal in the name of duty to the state, seen here in Senator Bird's arguments, see Genevieve Lloyd, "Selfhood, War and Masculinity," in *Feminist Challenges: Social and Political Theory,* ed. Carole Pateman and Elizabeth Gross (1986; reprint ed., Boston: Northeastern University Press, 1987), 63–76.

3. *Key to "Uncle Tom's Cabin,"* 143.

4. Weil, *Waiting for God,* 51.

5. As cited in Prior, "Mrs. Stowe's Uncle Tom," 649.

Chapter 6

1. Stowe regularly employed these standard nineteenth-century terms. *Quadroon* meant a person who was one-quarter of African-American descent; *octoroon* meant one-eighth. *Mulatto* referred to a person of mixed white and black ancestry.

2. Foster, *Rungless Ladder,* 31–32; Kirkham, *Building,* 98; *Key to "Uncle Tom's Cabin,"* 37–38.

3. Fisher, *Hard Facts,* 19, argues that, contrary to Russian formalist theorists who maintain that literature defamiliarizes, popular literary forms familiarize readers so as to change their ideas and attitudes, thus changing ideology.

4. *Key to "Uncle Tom's Cabin,"* 155.

5. Ibid., 155.

6. Eugene D. Genovese, "The Gospel in the Quarters," in *American Negro Slavery: A Modern Reader,* ed. Allen Weinstein et al., 3d ed. (1968; reprint ed., New York: Oxford University Press, 1979), 119, 135.

7. Evan Brandstadter, "Uncle Tom and Archy Moore," *American Quarterly* 26, no. 2 (May 1970):164–65; Kirkham, *Building*, 155, 233–44; Tremaine McDowell, "The Use of Negro Dialect by Harriet Beecher Stowe," *American Speech* 6 (June 1931): 322–26.

8. Gwin, *Black and White Women*, 23–25.

Chapter 7

1. Moers, "Mrs. Stowe's Vengeance," 25, and *Literary Women*, 56.

2. *Key to "Uncle Tom's Cabin,"* 34.

3. Brandstadter, "Uncle Tom," 165.

4. *Key to "Uncle Tom's Cabin,"* 1, v. See also Fields, *Life and Letters,* 271–72.

5. As cited in Wagenknecht, *Harriet Beecher Stowe*, 147, 161.

6. The *National Era* text and the book edition agree on chapter titles for chaps. 1–7, 9–23, and 40–45. Titles were lacking in the *Era* text for chaps. 24–39, which were supplied for the book publication. But the title for chap. 8, "Eliza's Escape," which is inaccurate, was supplied later—by whom is unclear. See Kirkham, *Building*, 166–67.

7. Murdoch, *Sovereignty of Good*, 66.

8. Fields, *Life and Letters*, 176.

9. On these Marxist concepts see Donovan, *Feminist Theory*, 72–73.

10. Tompkins, "Sentimental Power," 83, 97.

Chapter 8

1. *Key to "Uncle Tom's Cabin,"* 84.

2. Fields, *Life and Letters*, 177.

3. Burgess, "Making," 57.

4. The subtitle of Hannah Arendt's study of Nazi war criminal Adolf Eichmann, *Eichmann in Jerusalem: A Report on the Banality of Evil* (New York: Viking, 1963).

5. Elizabeth Ammons, "Stowe's Dream of the Mother-Savior: *Uncle Tom's Cabin* and American Women Writers before the 1920s," in *New Essays,* 164.

6. As cited in Harry S. Stout, *The New England Soul: Preaching and Religious Culture in Colonial New England* (New York: Oxford University Press, 1986), 367 n. 53. See also Crozier, *Novels,* 19–20.

7. Baldwin, "Everybody's Protest Novel," 28; Fiedler, *Love and Death,* 262.

8. Taylor, *Cavalier and Yankee,* 21.

9. See Donovan, *New England Local Color Literature,* 52–54.

10. Brown, "Getting in the Kitchen," 505, 511.

Chapter 9

1. Foster, *Rungless Ladder,* 51, 54; Kirkham, *Building,* 53–56.

2. Theodore R. Hovet, "Christian Revolution: Harriet Beecher Stowe's Response to Slavery and the Civil War," *New England Quarterly* 47, no. 4 (December 1974):527–49; Gossett, *"Uncle Tom's Cabin,"* 310–11; Fields, *Life and Letters,* 259, 271.

3. Terrell, *Harriet Beecher Stowe,* 19. See also Thomas Graham, "Harriet Beecher Stowe and the Question of Race," *New England Quarterly* 46, no. 4 (December 1973):614–22.

4. See Brock, *Journeys by Heart,* 9–14, on the contemporary abused child and the healing process.

5. *Key to "Uncle Tom's Cabin,"* 91–92.

6. Douglas, *Feminization,* 2, 12; Tompkins, "Sentimental Power," 85–86.

Chapter 10

1. Buell, *New England Literary Culture,* 186. Little Eva, of course, could also be seen to merit that distinction.

2. Virgil, *The Aeneid of Virgil,* trans. C. Day Lewis (New York: Doubleday Anchor, 1953), 138, ll. 295–301.

3. Taylor, *Cavalier and Yankee,* 309–10; see also Walter Benn Michaels, "Romance and Real Estate," *Raritan* 2 (Winter 1983):78–81.

4. Prior, "Mrs. Stowe's Uncle Tom," 650. Stowe's model for Tom's behavior may have come from testimony provided by Sarah Grimké in Weld's *American Slavery as It Is,* 24, which describes a Christian slave who is beaten to death for refusing to deny his religion (Yellin, "Doing It Herself," 95).

5. Sandra M. Gilbert and Susan Gubar, *The Madwoman in the Attic: The Woman Writer and the Nineteenth-Century Literary Imagination* (New Haven: Yale University Press, 1979), 534–35.

Selected Bibliography

Primary Works

Agnes of Sorrento. Boston: Ticknor and Fields, 1862.

The Chimney-Corner. Boston: Ticknor and Fields, 1868.

Dred: A Tale of the Great Dismal Swamp. Boston: Phillips, Sampson, 1856.

House and Home Papers. Boston: Ticknor and Fields, 1865.

The Key to "Uncle Tom's Cabin": Presenting the Original Facts and Documents upon Which the Story Is Founded. Boston: John P. Jewett; Cleveland: Jewett, Proctor & Worthington, 1853.

Lady Byron Vindicated. Boston: Fields, Osgood, 1870.

The Mayflower; or, Sketches of Scenes and Characters among the Descendants of the Pilgrims. New York: Harper & Brothers, 1843.

Men of Our Times; or, Leading Patriots of the Day. Hartford: Hartford Publishing Co., 1868.

The Minister's Wooing. New York: Derby and Jackson, 1859.

My Wife and I; or, Harry Henderson's History. New York: J. B. Ford, 1871.

Oldtown Fireside Stories. Boston: James R. Osgood, 1872.

Oldtown Folks. Boston: Fields, Osgood, 1869.

Palmetto Leaves. Boston: James R. Osgood, 1873.

The Pearl of Orr's Island: A Story of the Coast of Maine: Boston: Ticknor and Fields, 1862.

Pink and White Tyranny: A Society Novel. Boston: Roberts, 1871.

Poganuc People: Their Loves and Lives. New York: Fords, Howard, & Hulbert, 1878.

Religious Poems. Boston: Ticknor and Fields, 1867.

Sam Lawson's Oldtown Fireside Stories. Boston: Houghton, Mifflin, 1881.

Sunny Memories of Foreign Lands. Boston: Phillips, Sampson, 1854.

Selected Bibliography

Uncle Tom's Cabin; or Life among the Lowly. Boston: John P. Jewett; Cleveland, Ohio: Jewett, Proctor & Worthington, 1852.

We and Our Neighbors; or, The Records of an Unfashionable Street. New York: J. B. Ford, 1875.

Woman in Sacred History: A Series of Sketches Drawn from Scriptural, Historical and Legendary Sources. New York: J. B. Ford, 1874.

The Writings of Harriet Beecher Stowe. Cambridge: Riverside Press, 1896. 16 vols. Vol. 1, pp. liii–xciii, is a new introduction written by Stowe for this edition of *Uncle Tom's Cabin;* it cites numerous letters she received after the first publication.

Secondary Works

Books and Parts of Books

Adams, John R. *Harriet Beecher Stowe.* New York: Twayne, 1963. A short survey of Stowe's life and work, somewhat negative and condescending in tone.

Ammons, Elizabeth, ed. *Critical Essays on Harriet Beecher Stowe.* Boston: G. K. Hall, 1980. Includes excerpts from several reviews and essays on *Uncle Tom's Cabin.* Useful for the general reader.

Ashton, Jean W., comp. *Harriet Beecher Stowe: A Reference Guide.* Boston: G. K. Hall, 1977. The standard bibliography of secondary sources. Annotated.

Baldwin, James. "Everybody's Protest Novel." In *Notes of a Native Son,* 13–28. Boston: Beacon Press, 1955. Provocative, hostile reading of *Uncle Tom's Cabin,* marred by misogynist vituperation.

Braithwaite, William Hanley. "The Negro in American Literature." In *The New Negro,* edited by Alain Locke, 1925. Reprint. New York: Atheneum, 1969, 29–44. Sees *Uncle Tom's Cabin* as establishing powerful stereotypes that black authors had trouble overcoming.

Brooks, Van Wyck. *Literature in New England: The Flowering of New England, 1815–1865.* 1936. Reprint. Garden City, N.Y.: Garden City Publishing Co., 1944, 417–21. Brief but perceptive assessment of Stowe and *Uncle Tom's Cabin.*

Buell, Lawrence. *New England Literary Culture: From Revolution through Renaissance.* Cambridge: Cambridge University Press, 1986. Places *Uncle Tom's Cabin* in context of New England intellectual traditions; brief treatment of the novel but useful background about New England culture.

Cooke, Rose Terry. "Harriet Beecher Stowe." In *Our Famous Women,* by Elizabeth Stuart Phelps et al., 581–601. Hartford, Conn.: Worthington, 1884. A sentimental but contemporaneous sketch, probably based on an interview with Stowe, by an acquaintance.

Crozier, Alice C. *The Novels of Harriet Beecher Stowe.* New York: Oxford University Press, 1969. Sees *Uncle Tom's Cabin* as qualified expression of Edwardsean Calvinism, especially the doctrine of the holy affections. One of the first serious scholarly treatments of the novel; still an important study.

Crumpacker, Laurie. "Four Novels of Harriet Beecher Stowe: A Study in Nineteenth-Century Androgyny." In *American Novelists Revisited: Essays in Feminist Criticism,* ed. Fritz Fleischmann. Boston: G. K. Hall, 1982, 78–106. Studies "philosophy of domestic feminism" in *Uncle Tom's Cabin* in context of Stowe's evolving notions about women's roles seen in three subsequent novels.

Fiedler, Leslie A. *The Inadvertent Epic: From "Uncle Tom's Cabin" to "Roots."* New York: Simon & Schuster, 1979. Several quirky but provocative perceptions of the novel.

———. *Love and Death in the American Novel,* 260–66. New York: Criterion Books, 1960. One of the first positive twentieth-century reassessments of *Uncle Tom's Cabin,* "an astonishingly various and complex book."

Fields, Annie, ed. *Life and Letters of Harriet Beecher Stowe.* Boston: Houghton, Mifflin, 1898. Largely a collection of Stowe letters, this work remains one of the main biographical sources on the writer. Includes many revealing letters about the composition of *Uncle Tom's Cabin.* The editor's observations about Stowe's character are also useful.

Fisher, Philip. *Hard Facts: Setting and Form in the American Novel,* 87–127. New York: Oxford University Press, 1985. One of the most valuable contemporary reevaluations of the novel by a "new Americanist" critic. Places *Uncle Tom's Cabin* within the sentimentalist tradition and helps to explain the ideology of that tradition.

Foster, Charles H. *The Rungless Ladder: Harriet Beecher Stowe and New England Puritanism.* 1954. Reprint. New York: Cooper Square, 1970. Remains the standard study of Stowe's religious development; interprets her novels in terms of Edwardsean Calvinism and provides other useful background information about *Uncle Tom's Cabin.* Sees Stowe as a political radical.

Furnas, J. C. *Goodbye to Uncle Tom.* New York: William Sloan, 1956. A strange book written by a white man in a snide, sarcastic tone, which blames Stowe and *Uncle Tom's Cabin* for inculcating generations of

Americans with racist ideas and thereby perpetrating race problems in the United States.

Frederickson, George M. *The Black Image in the White Mind: The Debate on Afro-American Character and Destiny, 1817–1914.* New York: Harper, 1971. The most cogent discussion of the racial theories in *Uncle Tom's Cabin,* identifying the dominant concept as "romantic racialism" and rooting the idea in nineteenth-century ideology.

Gilbert, Sandra M., and Susan Gubar. *The Madwoman in the Attic: The Woman Writer and the Nineteenth-Century Imagination,* 533–35. New Haven: Yale University Press, 1979. Interesting discussion of Cassy as an archetypal "madwoman in the attic."

Gossett, Thomas F. *"Uncle Tom's Cabin" and American Culture.* Dallas: Southern Methodist University Press, 1985. One of the most useful background studies of the novel; provides a wealth of information about relevant nineteenth-century American cultural history. Especially valuable for its lengthy survey of critical reaction to the novel.

Gwin, Monrose C. *Black and White Women of the Old South.* Knoxville: University of Tennessee Press, 1985. Sees racist stereotypes in *Uncle Tom's Cabin* but identifies a "feminist subtext" in which black and white women ally in response to white "male-initiated crises."

Hildreth, Margaret Holbrook. *Harriet Beecher Stowe: A Bibliography.* Hamden, Conn.: Archon, 1976. The most complete primary bibliography, listing 139 English-language editions of the novel and translations in 59 languages. Includes secondary bibliography that is especially useful for its list of foreign critical works (untranslated) on *Uncle Tom's Cabin.*

Kemble, Fanny. *Journal of a Residence on a Georgian Plantation, 1838–1839,* edited by John A. Scott, Appendix A, 347–68. New York: Knopf, 1961. This unpublished letter to the editor of the London *Times,* written in 1853 but not published until 1863, verifies Stowe's depiction of slavery; if anything, Kemble remarks, Stowe understated the evils of the system.

Kirkham, E. Bruce. *The Building of "Uncle Tom's Cabin."* Knoxville: University of Tennessee Press, 1977. Probably the single most valuable secondary work on the novel for the scholar. Provides extensive background information on its composition, arguing that it went through three revisions: an original draft, the revised text sent to the *National Era,* and the text prepared for the first book edition. (Unfortunately only nine manuscript pages remain from any of these versions.)

Lang, Amy Schrager. *Prophetic Woman: Anne Hutchinson and the Problem of Dissent in the Literature of New England,* 193–213. Berkeley: University of California Press, 1987. Links the novel to the tradition of female antinomianism in America but sees Stowe electing a religious rather than a political solution in *Uncle Tom's Cabin*. Also includes useful discussion of Jonathan Edwards's theology.

Lynn, Kenneth S. Introduction to *Uncle Tom's Cabin: Or, Life among the Lowly*. Cambridge, Mass.: Harvard University Press, Belknap Press, 1962. One of the first serious scholarly reassessments in the twentieth century. Places the novel in the tradition of realism.

Maclean, Grace Edith. *"Uncle Tom's Cabin" in Germany*. New York: D. Appleton, 1910. Traces the extensive influence of the novel in Germany.

Moers, Ellen. *Literary Women, 55–59, 129–30*. Garden City, N.Y.: Anchor/ Doubleday, 1977. Brief but perceptive comments by pioneer feminist critic.

Papashvily, Helen Waite. *All the Happy Endings: A Study of the Domestic Novel in America, the Women Who Wrote It, the Women Who Read It, in the Nineteenth century, 70–77*. New York: Harper, 1956. Locates the novel in the sentimentalist tradition, which she sees as a covert expression of feminist subversion.

Reynolds, Moira Reynolds. *"Uncle Tom's Cabin" and Mid-Nineteenth Century United States: Pen and Conscience*. Jefferson, N.C.: McFarland, 1985. Useful background information for the general reader.

Reynolds, David S. *Beneath the American Renaissance: The Subversive Imagination in the Age of Emerson and Melville, 74–79*. New York: Knopf, 1988. An important study by a new Americanist critic that recognizes the power and moral depth of *Uncle Tom's Cabin* but criticizes its failure to "fuse" its "warring elements," thereby falling short of major literary status. Argues that the novel defuses its subversive potential with conventional solutions.

Rourke, Constance Mayfield. *Trumpets of Jubilee*. New York: Harcourt, Brace, 1927. Important early twentieth-century study of Stowe and the novel, which is interpreted in biographical terms as an expression of the author's own bondage and rebellion.

Showalter, Elaine. "Piecing and Writing." In *The Poetics of Gender,* edited by Nancy K. Miller, 222–47. New York: Columbia University Press, 1986. Sees *Uncle Tom's Cabin* as structured according to the pattern in the popular log cabin quilt.

Spillers, Hortense J. "Changing the Letter: The Yokes, the Jokes of Discourse, or, Mrs. Stowe, Mr. Reed." In *Slavery and the Literary Imagination,* Selected Papers from the English Institute, 1987, n.s., no. 13, pp. 25–61. Baltimore: Johns Hopkins University Press, 1989. Postmodernist approach that compares *Uncle Tom's Cabin* with Ishmael Reed's burlesque of it, *Flight to Canada* (1976). Provocative insights; objects to Stowe's use of a black man as a sacrificial victim and suggests Eva represents repressed white female desire. Both Tom and Eva are doomed because they are threats to the ethos of white patriarchy.

Stowe, Charles Edward. *Life of Harriet Beecher Stowe: Compiled from Her Letters and Journals.* Boston: Houghton Mifflin, 1889. Apparently written in collaboration with the author herself, this work has "the force of an autobiography" (as she notes in the preface). The most detailed and valuable of the early biographies, especially for its material on Harriet's childhood and early education. Includes transcripts of numerous letters, many reproduced in Annie Fields's *Life and Letters.*

Stowe, Charles Edward, and Lyman Beecher Stowe. *Harriet Beecher Stowe: The Story of Her Life.* Boston: Houghton Mifflin, 1911. A few details added to the 1889 biography but not as thorough a study.

Stowe, Lyman Beecher. *Saints, Sinners, and Beechers,* 154–235. Indianapolis: Bobbs-Merrill, 1934. Popular biography with chapter on Harriet.

Sundquist, Eric J. *New Essays on "Uncle Tom's Cabin."* Cambridge: Cambridge University Press, 1986. One of the most important new studies of the novel; includes essays by Sundquist, Richard Yarborough, Jean Fagan Yellin, Karen Halttunen, Robert B. Stepto, and Elizabeth Ammons. Somewhat of a new Americanist cast, the essays generally evince respect for Stowe and the novel, but Yarborough is critical of her racial attitudes and of the baneful influence he sees the novel as having had on the black literary tradition. Yellin is also critical, seeing *Uncle Tom's Cabin* as finally a conservative work. Halttunen analyzes the gothic features in the novel; Stepto connects it to certain slave narratives; and Ammons locates it within a matriarchal utopian tradition in American women's literature. Sundquist's introduction also has valuable insights.

Taylor, William R. *Cavalier and Yankee: The Old South and American National Character,* 308–13. New York: Braziller, 1961. Connects *Uncle Tom's Cabin* to the tradition of the antebellum southern plantation novel.

Terrell, Mary Church. *Harriet Beecher Stowe: An Appreciation.* Washington, D.C.: Murray Brothers, 1911. A short, admiring, somewhat sentimental biography by a leading turn-of-the-century black activist.

Tompkins, Jane P. "Sentimental Power: *Uncle Tom's Cabin* and the Politics of Literary History." In *The New Feminist Criticism: Essays on Women, Literature, and Theory,* edited by Elaine Showalter, 81–104. New York: Pantheon, 1985. Originally appeared in *Glyph* (1978); also in *Sensational Designs: The Cultural Work of American Fiction, 1790–1860,* New York: Oxford University Press, 1985. A key new Americanist interpretation of the novel, seeing it as the "summa theologica of nineteenth-century America's religion of domesticity." Important revisionist understanding of the novel's religious themes.

Wagenknecht, Edward. *Harriet Beecher Stowe: the Known and the Unknown.* New York: Oxford University Press, 1965. A biographical study. Some insights not available elsewhere but at times condescending toward its subject.

Weld, Theodore. *American Slavery as It Is: Testimony of a Thousand Witnesses.* New York: American Anti-Slavery Society, 1839. Important source used by Stowe for the novel.

Wilson, Edmund. *Patriotic Gore: Studies in the Literature of the American Civil War.* New York: Oxford University Press, 1962. One of first twentieth-century reassessments; evinces grudging but condescending admiration for the work.

Wilson, Forrest. *Crusader in Crinoline: The Life of Harriet Beecher Stowe.* Philadelphia: Lippincott, 1941. Despite having been written nearly half a century ago, this remains the standard biography. Thorough, detailed, and balanced, the work is affectionately respectful toward its subject.

Yellin, Jean Fagan. *The Intricate Knot: Black Figures in American Literature, 1776–1863.* New York: New York University Press, 1972. Considers the novel in the context of abolitionist debate, seeing it as a response to the tactical issue of the use of violence or nonviolence. Useful survey of early black response to the novel.

Journal Articles

Ammons, Elizabeth. "Heroines in *Uncle Tom's Cabin*." *American Literature* 49, no. 2 (May 1977):161–79. First to recognize important cultural feminist theme in *Uncle Tom's Cabin*—that feminine values are seen as politically redemptive.

Brandstadter, Evan. "Uncle Tom and Archy Moore: The Antislavery Novel as Ideological Symbol." *American Quarterly* 26, no. 2 (May 1974):160–75. Compares Richard Hildreth's antislavery novel *Archy Moore* (1836) with *Uncle Tom's Cabin,* suggesting that latter's greater success was due to its softer political message.

Brown, Gillian. "Getting in the Kitchen with Dinah: Domestic Politics in *Uncle Tom's Cabin*." *American Quarterly* 36, no. 4 (Fall 1984):502–23. A socialist feminist approach. One of the most important recent analyses. Argues Stowe envisaged replacing the capitalist market economy with a matriarchal domestic economy, seeing the novel as a radical critique of capitalist patriarchy.

Burgess, Anthony. "Making de White Boss Frown." *Encounter* 27, no. 1 (July 1966):54–58. Positive appreciation of the work by a contemporary British novelist.

Duvall, Severn. "Uncle Tom's Cabin: The Sinister Side of the Patriarchy." *New England Quarterly* 36, no. 1 (March 1963):3–22. Sees novel as attack on proslavery theory that the system was a benign familial arrangement.

Selected Bibliography

Graham, Thomas. "Harriet Beecher Stowe and the Question of Race." *New England Quarterly* 46, no. 4 (December 1973):614–22. Defends Stowe against Furnas's attack in *Goodbye to Uncle Tom;* says she was not a racist and was aware of the subtleties of racial oppression.

Hale, Nancy. "What God Was Writing." *Texas Quarterly* 1, no. 2 (Spring 1958):35–40. Interesting Jungian interpretation of the novel, seeing its tensions as manifesting the struggle of the ego to escape from the unconscious. Whites such as Eva and Marie represent rationalist principles that would repress the dark realms of the psyche. Uncle Tom is a God archetype.

Haley, Alex. "In 'Uncle Tom' Are Our Guilt and Our Hope." *New York Times Magazine,* 1 March 1964, 23, 90. Recognizes irony in current use of "Uncle Tom" as negative epithet; respects novel for helping to end slavery.

Hovet, Theodore R. "Christian Revolution: Harriet Beecher Stowe's Response to Slavery and the Civil War." *New England Quarterly* 47, no. 4 (December 1974):527–49. Traces Stowe's political and religious attitudes, seeing her finally as a religious revolutionary.

Jaffe, Adrian. "Uncle Tom in the Penal Colony: Heine's View of *Uncle Tom's Cabin.*" *American German Review* 19 (February 1953):5–6. Short but provocative comparison between *Uncle Tom's Cabin* and Kafka's "In the Penal Colony."

Klingberg, Frank L. "Harriet Beecher Stowe and Social Reform in England." *American Historical Review* 43 (April 1938):542–52. Traces influence of *Uncle Tom's Cabin* on working-class reform movements in England.

Levin, David. "American Fiction as Historical Evidence: Reflections on *Uncle Tom's Cabin.*" *Negro American Literature Forum* 5 (Winter 1972):132–36, 154. An admiring reassessment of the work, stressing its documentary value and defending it against attacks by James Baldwin and others.

Maurice, Arthur Bartlett. "Famous Novels and Their Contemporary Critics." *Bookman* 17 (March 1903):23–30. A useful selection of early reviews.

McDowell, Tremaine. "The Use of Negro Dialect by Harriet Beecher Stowe." *American Speech* 6 (June 1931):322–26. Says she was careless and inaccurate in *Uncle Tom's Cabin* but achieved "excellent effects" nevertheless.

Moers, Ellen. "Mrs. Stowe's Vengeance." *New York Review of Books,* 3 September 1970, 25–32. Review of Alice C. Crozier, *The Novels of Harriet Beecher Stowe* (1969), that reassesses the novel positively.

Prior, Moody. "Mrs. Stowe's Uncle Tom." *Critical Inquiry* 5, no. 4 (Summer 1979):635–50. Refutes charge that Stowe was a racist; reinterprets novel in terms of contemporary existentialism, seeing Tom as a hero in that he affirms his humanity by refusing to capitulate under torture.

Index

Index

Fisher, Philip, 9, 22–23, 31
Foster, Charles H., 7, 50
Frederickson, George, 19
Fugitive Slave Law, 4–5, 34, 44, 61, 65, 79

Gandhi, Mahatma, 14
Garrison, William Lloyd, 4, 18
Genovese, Eugene, 56
Gogol, Nikolai: *Dead Souls*, 9
Grimké, Sarah: *Letters on Equality*, 5
Gwin, Monrose, 58–59

Haley, Alex, 19
Harper, Frances E. W., 18–19
Heine, Heinrich, 16
Henson, Josiah, 8, 50–51
Howells, William Dean, 17
Hughes, Langston, 19
Hugo, Victor, 16

James, Henry, 20
Jameson, Fredric, 25–26
Johnson, James Weldon, 19

King, Martin Luther, Jr., 14–15
Kinmont, Alexander, 19

Lincoln, Abraham, 11
Love, redemptive, 14–15, 45–47, 67, 96–99, 112–13
Lowell, James Russell, 16
Lynn, Kenneth, 21

Marx, Karl, and Friedrich Engels, 25, 41; *The Communist Manifesto*, 3, 89–90
Marxism, 14, 25–26, 36, 41–42, 68, 89–91
Matthiessen, F. O., 20
Maxfield, E. K., 20
Melville, Herman: "Benito Cerino," 21; *Moby-Dick*, 14, 22, 113

Moers, Ellen, 23, 60
Murdoch, Iris, 64

National Era, 30
Natural rights doctrine, 3, 65–66
New Americanist criticism, 21–23
Northrup, Solomon, 8

Papashvily, Helen, 23
Parrington, Vernon, 20
Plantation novels, 8, 79, 105
Prior, Moody, 107
Problem of evil, 12, 33–39, 56, 76, 90, 93; economic roots of, 40–42, 89, 105

Quinn, Arthur Hobson, 20

Racial theories, 19–20, 50, 54–56, 79, 81, 92, 94–96
Realism, 9–10, 49, 63–64, 71
Revolution of 1848, 3, 88
Reynolds, David S., 23–24

Sand, George, 16
Sartre, Jean-Paul, 46
Scott, Sir Walter, 9
Sentimentalism, 8–9, 22–23, 99
Showalter, Elaine, 24, 30
Simon Magus / Faustus, 103, 109
Slavery, 3–5, 38, 62, 74–75
Solomon, Maynard, 26
Solzhenitsyn, Alexandr, 107
Spiller, Robert E., 20
Spillers, Hortense, 24, 58, 78
Stowe, Charles, 29
Stowe, Harriet Beecher, 3–4, 5–7, 19, 31, 62, 66, 74, 91, 97, 116

WORKS:
"Can the Immortality of the Soul Be Proved by the Light of Nature?" 31
Dred, 91

135

"Isabelle and Her Sister Kate, and Their Sister," 81
The Key to "Uncle Tom's Cabin," 43, 51, 73, 96
The Minister's Wooing, 9, 58
Oldtown Folks, 9, 53
The Pearl of Orr's Island, 9
See also *Uncle Tom's Cabin*

Sundquist, Eric, 22

Terrell, Mary Church, 19, 95
Tolstoi, Leo, 16
Tompkins, Jane, 22, 69, 99–100
Tourgée, Albion W., 17
Turgenev, Ivan, 16

Uncle Tom's Cabin: antithetical characters in, 13, 48, 52, 58, 63, 66, 72, 79, 91, 95, 101; black criticism of, 17–20, 95; dialect in, 57–58; literary traditions in, 8–10; religious background, 7–8; sources, 8; structure, 13, 24, 30–33, 48,
70, 115; style, 29–30, 48–50, 61–62; themes, *see* capitalism; love, redemptive; problem of evil; utopian ideals

Underground railroad, 44, 65, 66, 88

Utopian ideals, 26, 55–57, 68, 82, 98, 106, 116

Van Doren, Carl, 20
Virgil: *Aeneid,* 104

Wagenknecht, Edward, 21
Weil, Simone, 45
Weld, Theodore: *American Slavery as It Is,* 8
Whittier, John Greenleaf, 16
Wilson, Edmund, 20
Women's rights movement, 4–5
Woodhull, Victoria, 89
Wright, Henry C., 18

Yellin, Jean Fagan, 24

The Author

Josephine Donovan received her Ph.D. and M.A. in comparative literature from the University of Wisconsin-Madison and her B.A. from Bryn Mawr College. She is professor of English at the University of Maine and the author of several studies of American women's literature, including *After the Fall: The Demeter-Persephone Myth in Edith Wharton, Willa Cather, and Ellen Glasgow* (1989); *New England Local Color Literature: A Women's Tradition* (1983); which includes a chapter on Stowe; and *Sarah Orne Jewett* (1980). She is also the author of *Feminist Theory: The Intellectual Traditions of American Feminism* (1985) and edited *Feminist Literary Criticism: Explorations in Theory* (1975), the second edition of which appeared in 1989. Her articles include "Harriet Beecher Stowe's Feminism," *American Transcendental Quarterly* 47–48 (Summer–Fall 1980): 141–57. She lives in Portsmouth, New Hampshire.